D0891592

PEOPLE LIVE HERE
SELECTED POEMS 1949-1983

FINKELSTEIN
MEMORIAL LIBRARY
SPRING VALLEY, N. Y.

PEOPLE
LIVE
HERE

SELECTED POEMS 1949-1983

LOUIS SIMPSON

BOA EDITIONS, LTD. ▪ BROCKPORT, NEW YORK ▪ 1983

84–29891

Grateful acknowledgement is made to the editors and publishers of the following publications in which the poems in this book were originally published and/or collected:
The Fine Editions Press, for poems from *The Arrivistes: Poems 1940-1949*, 1949; Charles Scribner's Sons, for poems from *Good News of Death and Other Poems in Poets of Today II*, 1955; *Wesleyan University Press, for poems from A Dream of Governors*, 1959; Wesleyan University Press, for poems from *At the End of the Open Road*, 1963; Harcourt Brace Jovanovitch, for poems from *Selected Poems*, 1965; Harper & Row, Publishers, for poems from *Adventures of the Letter I*, 1971; William Morrow & Co., Inc., for poems from *Searching for the Ox*, 1976; BOA Editions, Ltd., for poems from *Armidale*, 1979; Franklin Watts, for Poems from *Caviare at the Funeral*, 1980; reprinted by permission of Franklin Watts, Inc.; *The Hudson review*, for "Physical Universe"; *The Iowa Review*, for "Quiet Desperation"; and *Occident*, the University of California, for "The Fleet for Tsushima." "The Sound of Words for Their Own Sake—An Afterword" originally appeared in *The New York Times Book Review* and is reprinted here with their permission.

Copyright © 1983 by Louis Simpson. All rights reserved. Printed in the United States of America. Except in the case of brief quotations in reviews, no part of this publication may be reproduced or transmitted in any form or by any means without written permission from the publisher. All inquiries should be addressed to: BOA Editions, Ltd., 92 Park Avenue, Brockport, New York 14420.

ISBN 0-918526-42-6 Cloth
ISBN 0-918526-43-4 Paper

Library of Congress Catalogue Card Number: 83-071364

Publications by BOA Editions, Ltd., are made possible in part with the assistance of grants from the Literature Program of the New York State Council on the Arts and the Literature Program of the National Endowment for the Arts, a Federal Agency.

Designed and typeset at Visual Studies Workshop, Rochester, New York.

First Edition: December, 1983

BOA Editions, Ltd.
A. Poulin, Jr., President
92 Park Avenue
Brockport, New York 14420

CONTENTS

A NOTE TO THE READER

This is not the usual chronological arrangement—poems selected from the author's first book followed by poems from the second, and so on. Instead I have selected poems from all my books and placed them in groups. There is an opening section of "Songs and Lyrics"—in other sections the poems are centered around an idea. I believe that this arrangement shows the nature of my writing more clearly than has appeared up to now in separate books.

It follows that poems in contrasting forms may stand side by side—an early poem in meter and rhyme next to a more recent poem written in free form. In general, however, my early poems are located in the two opening sections.

Readers who wish to know when and where the poems were first published in books may find that information in the "Chronology of the Poems" on pages 205-208 of this book.

L.S.

I

SONGS AND LYRICS

ROUGH WINDS DO SHAKE

Rough winds do shake
                  do shake
                                    the darling buds of May
The darling buds
                  rose buds
                            the winds do shake
That are her breasts.
Those darling buds, dew-tipped, her sighing moods do shake.

She is sixteen
                  sixteen
                          and her young lust
Is like a thorn
                hard thorn
                          among the pink
Of her soft nest.
Upon this thorn she turns, for love's incessant sake.

Her heart will break
                  will break
                              unless she may
Let flow her blood
                  red blood
                          to ease the ache
Where she is pressed.
Then she'll lie still, asleep, who now lies ill, awake.

Well, I have seen
                  have seen
                        one come to joust
Who has a horn
                sweet horn,
                        and spear to sink
Before he rests.
When such young buds are torn, the best true loves they make.

AS BIRDS ARE FITTED TO THE BOUGHS

As birds are fitted to the boughs
That blossom on the tree
And whisper when the south wind blows—
So was my love to me.

And still she blossoms in my mind
And whispers softly, though
The clouds are fitted to the wind,
The wind is to the snow.

THE CUSTOM OF THE WORLD

O, we loved long and happily, God knows!
The ocean danced, the green leaves tossed, the air
Was filled with petals, and pale Venus rose
When we began to kiss. Kisses brought care,
And closeness caused the taking off of clothes.
O, we loved long and happily, God knows!

"The watchdogs are asleep, the doormen doze...."
We huddled in the corners of the stair,
And then we climbed it. What had we to lose?
What would we gain? The best way to compare
And quickest, was by taking off our clothes.
O, we loved long and happily, God knows!

Between us two a silent treason grows,
Our pleasures have been changed into despair.
Wild is the wind, from a cold country blows,
In which these tender blossoms disappear.
And did this come of taking off our clothes?
O, we loved long and happily, God knows!

Mistress, my song is drawing to a close.
Put on your rumpled skirt and comb your hair,
And when we meet again let us suppose
We never loved or ever naked were.
For though this nakedness was good, God knows,
The custom of the world is wearing clothes.

BIRCH

Birch tree, you remind me
Of a room filled with breathing,
The sway and whisper of love.

She slips off her shoes;
Unzips her skirt; arms raised,
Unclasps an earring, and the other.

Just so the sallow trunk
Divides, and the branches
Are pale and smooth.

THE TROIKA

Troika, troika! The snow moon
whirls through the forest.

Where lamplight like a knife
gleams through a door, I see two graybeards bending.
They're playing chess, it seems. And then one rises
and stands in silence. Does he hear me passing?

Troika, troika! In the moonlight
his spirit hears my spirit passing.

I whip the horses on. The houses vanish.
The moon looks over fields
littered with debris. And there in trenches
the guardsmen stand, wind fluttering their rags.

And there were darker fields without a moon.
I walk across a field, bound on an errand.
The errand's forgotten—something depended on it.
A nightmare! I have lost my father's horses!

I held the bird—it vanished with a cry,
and on a branch a girl sat sideways, combing
her long black hair. The dew
shone on her lips; her breasts were white as roses.

Troika, troika! Three white horses,
a whip of silver, and my father's sleigh...

When morning breaks, the sea
gleams through the branches,
and the white bird, enchanted,
is flying through the world, across the sea.

MY FATHER IN THE NIGHT COMMANDING NO

My father in the night commanding No
Has work to do. Smoke issues from his lips;
    He reads in silence.
The frogs are croaking and the streetlamps glow.

And then my mother winds the gramophone;
The Bride of Lammermoor begins to shriek—
    Or reads a story
About a prince, a castle, and a dragon.

The moon is glittering above the hill.
I stand before the gateposts of the King—
    So runs the story—
Of Thule, at midnight when the mice are still.

And I have been in Thule! It has come true—
The journey and the danger of the world,
    All that there is
To bear and to enjoy, endure and do.

Landscapes, seascapes ... where have I been led?
The names of cities—Paris, Venice, Rome—
    Held out their arms.
A feathered god, seductive, went ahead.

Here is my house. Under a red rose tree
A child is swinging; another gravely plays.
    They are not surprised
That I am here; they were expecting me.

And yet my father sits and reads in silence,
My mother sheds a tear, the moon is still,
    And the dark wind
Is murmuring that nothing ever happens.

Beyond his jurisdiction as I move
Do I not prove him wrong? And yet, it's true
    They will not change
There, on the stage of terror and of love.

The actors in that playhouse always sit
In fixed positions—father, mother, child
    With painted eyes.
How sad it is to be a little puppet!

Their heads are wooden. And you once pretended
To understand them! Shake them as you will,
    They cannot speak.
Do what you will, the comedy is ended.

Father, why did you work? Why did you weep,
Mother? Was the story so important?
    "Listen!" the wind
Said to the children, and they fell asleep.

THE RIDERS HELD BACK

One morning, as we travelled in the fields
    Of air and dew
With trumpets, and above the painted shields
    The banners flew,

We came upon three ladies, wreathed in roses,
    Where, hand in hand,
They danced—three slender, gentle, naked ladies,
    All in a woodland.

They'd been to the best schools in Italy;
    Their legs were Greek,
Their collarbones, as fine as jewelry,
    They eyes, antique.

"Why do lambs skip and shepherds shout 'Ut hoy!'?
    Why do you dance?"
Said one "It is an intellectual joy,
    The Renaissance.

"As do the stars in heaven, ruled by Three,
    We twine and move.
It is the music of Astronomy,
    Not men, we love.

"And as we dance, the beasts and flowers do;
    The fields of wheat
Sway like our arms; the curving hills continue
    The curves of our feet.

"Here Raphael comes to paint; the thrushes flute
    To Petrarch's pen.
But Michael is not here, who carved the brute
    Unfinished men."

They danced again, and on the mountain heights
    There seemed to rise
Towers and ramparts glittering with lights,
    Like Paradise.

How the bright morning passed, I cannot say.
    We woke and found
The dancers gone; and heard, far, far away
    The trumpet sound.

We galloped to it. In the forest then
    Banners and shields
Were strewn like leaves; and there were many slain
    In the dark fields.

LUMINOUS NIGHT

I love the dark race of poets,
And yet there is also happiness.
Happiness . . .

If I can stand it, I can stand anything.
Luminous night, let fall your pearls!
Wind, toss the sodden boughs!

Then let the birch trees shine
Like crystal. Light the boughs!
We can live here, Cristina,

We can live here,
In this house, among these trees,
This world so many have left.

EARLY IN THE MORNING

Early in the morning
The dark Queen said,
"The trumpets are warning
There's trouble ahead."
Spent with carousing,
With wine-soaked wits,
Antony drowsing
Whispered, "It's
Too cold a morning
To get out of bed."

The army's retreating,
The fleet had fled,
Caesar is beating
His drums through the dead.
"Antony, horses!
We'll get away,
Gather our forces
For another day...."
"It's a cold morning,"
Antony said.

Caesar Augustus
Cleared his phlegm.
"Corpses disgust us.
Cover them."
Caesar Augustus
In his time lay
Dying, and just as
Cold as they,
On the cold morning
Of a cold day.

A DREAM OF GOVERNORS

The deepest dream is of mad governors.
—Mark Van Doren

The Knight from the world's end
Cut off the dragon's head.
The monster's only friend,
The Witch, insulting, fled.
The Knight was crowned, and took
His Lady. Good and gay,
They lived in a picture-book
Forever and a day.

Or else: When he had sat
So long, the King was old
And ludicrous and fat.
At feasts when poets told
How he had shed the blood
Of dragons long ago
He thought, Have I done good
To hear that I did so?

The chorus in a play
Declaimed: "The soul does well
Keeping the middle way."
He thought, That city fell;
Man's life is founded on
Folly at the extreme;
When all is said and done
The City is a dream.

At night the King alone
Went to the dragon's cave.
In moonlight on a stone
The Witch sat by the grave.
He grasped her by the hand
And said, "Grant what I ask.
Bring evil on the land
That I may have a task!"

24

The Queen has heard his tread;
She shuts the picture-book.
The King stands by the bed.
In silence as they look
Into each other's eyes
They see a buried thing
That creeps, begins to rise,
And spreads the dragon's wing.

THE GOODNIGHT

He stood still by her bed
Watching his daughter breathe,
The dark and silver head,
The fingers curled beneath,
And thought: Though she may have
Intelligence and charm
And luck, they will not save
Her life from every harm.

The lives of children are
Dangerous to their parents
With fire, water, air,
And other accidents;
And some, for a child's sake,
Anticipating doom,
Empty the world to make
The world safe as a room.

Who could endure the pain
That was Laocoön's?
Twisting, he saw again
In the same coil his sons.
Plumed in his father's skill,
Young Icarus flew higher
Toward the sun, until
He fell in rings of fire.

A man who cannot stand
Children's perilous play,
With lifted voice and hand
Drives the children away.
Out of sight, out of reach,
The tumbling children pass;
He sits on an empty beach,
Holding an empty glass.

Who said that tenderness
Will turn the heart to stone?
May I endure her weakness
As I endure my own.
Better to say goodnight
To breathing flesh and blood
Each night as though the night
Were always only good.

THE CRADLE TRAP

A bell and rattle,
a smell of roses,
a leather Bible,
and angry voices...

They say, I love you.
They shout, You must!
The light is telling
terrible stories.

But night at the window
whispers, Never mind.
Be true, be true
to your own strange kind.

THE MORNING LIGHT

In the morning light a line
Stretches forever. There my unlived life
Rises, and I resist,
Clinging to the steps of the throne.

Day lifts the darkness from the hills,
A bright blade cuts the reeds,
And my life, pitilessly demanding,
Rises forever in the morning light.

THE PIHIS

Since first I read in *Zone*
what Apollinaire says of the pihis,
"They have one wing only and fly in a couple" —

I have heard their cries at midnight
and seen the shadows of those passionate
generations of the moon.

TRASIMENO

When Hannibal defeated the Roman army
he stopped at Trasimeno.

That day, and the next, he marched no further.
His tent lay in the moonlight,

his sword shone in the moonlight,
what thought kept him from moving, no one knows.

Stranger, when you go to Rome,
when you have placed your hand in the gargoyle's mouth,

and walked in the alleys . . .
when you have satisfied your hunger for stone,

at night you will return to the trees
and the ways of the barbarians,

hands, eyes, voices, ephemera,
shadows of the African horsemen.

THE SILENT PIANO

We have lived like civilized people.
O ruins, traditions!

And we have seen the barbarians,
breakers of sculpture and glass.

And now we talk of "the inner life,"
and I ask myself, where is it?

Not here, in these streets and houses,
so I think it must be found

in indolence, pure indolence,
an ocean of darkness,

in silence, an arm of the moon,
a hand that enters slowly.

                   *

I am reminded of a story
Camus tells, of a man in prison camp.

He had carved a piano keyboard
with a nail on a piece of wood.

And sat there playing the piano.
This music was made entirely of silence.

THE PEAT-BOG MAN

He was one of the consorts of the moon,
and went with the goddess in a cart.

Wherever he went there would be someone,
a few of the last of the old religion.

Here the moon passes behind a cloud.
Fifteen centuries pass,

then one of the bog-peat cutters
digs up the man—with the rope

that ends in a noose at the throat—
a head squashed like a pumpkin.

Yet, there is delicacy in the features
and a peaceful expression . . .

that in Spring the flower comes forth
with a music of pipes and dancing.

II

THE FIGHTING IN EUROPE

CARENTAN O CARENTAN

Trees in the old days used to stand
And shape a shady lane
Where lovers wandered hand in hand
Who came from Carentan.

This was the shining green canal
Where we came two by two
Walking at combat-interval.
Such trees we never knew.

The day was early June, the ground
Was soft and bright with dew.
Far away the guns did sound,
But here the sky was blue.

The sky was blue, but there a smoke
Hung still above the sea
Where the ships together spoke
To towns we could not see.

Could you have seen us through a glass
You would have said a walk
Of farmers out to turn the grass,
Each with his own hay-fork.

The watchers in their leopard suits
Waited till it was time,
And aimed between the belt and boot
And let the barrel climb.

I must lie down at once, there is
A hammer at my knee.
And call it death or cowardice,
Don't count again on me.

Everything's all right, Mother,
Everyone gets the same
At one time or another.
It's all in the game.

I never strolled, nor ever shall,
Down such a leafy lane.
I never drank in a canal,
Nor ever shall again.

There is a whistling in the leaves
And it is not the wind,
The twigs are falling from the knives
That cut men to the ground.

Tell me, Master-Sergeant,
The way to turn and shoot.
But the Sergeant's silent
That taught me how to do it.

O Captain, show us quickly
Our place upon the map.
But the Captain's sickly
And taking a long nap.

Lieutenant, what's my duty,
My place in the platoon?
He too's a sleeping beauty,
Charmed by that strange tune.

Carentan O Carentan
Before we met with you
We never yet had lost a man
Or known what death could do.

MEMORIES OF A LOST WAR

The guns know what is what, but underneath
In fearful file
We go around burst boots and packs and teeth
That seem to smile.

The scene jags like a strip of celluloid,
A mortar fires,
Cinzano falls, Michelin is destroyed,
The man of tires.

As darkness drifts like fog in from the sea
Somebody says
"We're digging in." Look well, for this may be
The last of days.

Hot lightnings stitch the blind eye of the moon,
The thunder's blunt.
We sleep. Our dreams pass in a faint platoon
Toward the front.

Sleep well, for you are young. Each tree and bush
Drips with sweet dew,
And earlier than morning June's cool hush
Will waken you.

The riflemen will wake and hold their breath.
Through they may bleed
They will be proud a while of something death
Still seems to need.

THE BATTLE

Helmet and rifle, pack and overcoat
Marched through a forest. Somewhere up ahead
Guns thudded. Like the circle of a throat
The night on every side was turning red.

They halted and they dug. They sank like moles
Into the clammy earth between the trees.
And soon the sentries, standing in their holes,
Felt the first snow. Their feet began to freeze.

At dawn the first shell landed with a crack.
Then shells and bullets swept the icy woods.
This lasted many days. The snow was black.
The corpses stiffened in their scarlet hoods.

Most clearly of that battle I remember
The tiredness in eyes, how hands looked thin
Around a cigarette, and the bright ember
Would pulse with all the life there was within.

THE HEROES

I dreamed of war-herocs, of wounded war-heroes
With just enough of their charms shot away
To make them more handsome. The women moved nearer
To touch their brave wounds and their hair streaked with gray.

I saw them in long ranks ascending the gang-planks;
The girls with the doughnuts were cheerful and gay.
They minded their manners and muttered their thanks;
The Chaplain advised them to watch and to pray.

They shipped these rapscallions, these sea-sick battalions
To a patriotic and picturesque spot;
They gave them new bibles and marksmen's medallions,
Compasses, maps, and committed the lot.

A fine dust has settled on all that scrap metal.
The heroes were packaged and sent home in parts
To pluck at a poppy and sew on a petal
And count the long night by the stroke of their hearts.

THE ASH AND THE OAK

When men discovered freedom first
The fighting was on foot,
They were encouraged by their thirst
And promises of loot,
And when it feathered and bows boomed
Their virtue was a root.

O the ash and the oak and the willow tree
And green grows the grass on the infantry!

At Malplaquet and Waterloo
They were polite and proud,
They primed their guns with billets-doux
And, as they fired, bowed.
At Appomattox too, it seems
Some things were understood.

O the ash and the oak and the willow tree
And green grows the grass on the infantry!

But at Verdun and at Bastogne
There was a great recoil,
The blood was bitter to the bone
The trigger to the soul,
And death was nothing if not dull,
A hero was a fool.

O the ash and the oak and the willow tree
And that's an end of the infantry!

I DREAMED THAT IN A CITY DARK AS PARIS

I dreamed that in a city dark as Paris
I stood alone in a deserted square.
The night was trembling with a violet
Expectancy. At the far edge it moved
And rumbled; on that flickering horizon
The guns were pumping color in the sky.

There was the Front. But I was lonely here,
Left behind, abandoned by the army.
The empty city and the empty square
Was my inhabitation, my unrest.
The helmet with its vestige of a crest,
The rifle in my hands, long out of date,
The belt I wore, the trailing overcoat
And hobnail boots, were those of a *poilu*.
I was the man, as awkward as a bear.

Over the rooftops where cathedrals loomed
In speaking majesty, two aeroplanes,
Forlorn as birds, appeared. Then growing large,
the German *Taube* and the *Nieuport Scout*,
They chased each other tumbling through the sky,
Till one streamed down on fire to the earth.

These wars have been so great, they are forgotten
Like the Egyptian dynasts. My confrere
In whose thick boots I stood, were you amazed
To wander through my brain four decades later
As I have wandered in a dream through yours?

The violence of waking life disrupts
The order of our death. Strange dreams occur,
For dreams are licensed as they never were.

THE BIRD

"Ich wünscht', ich wäre ein Vöglein,"
Sang Heinrich, "I would fly
Across the sea ..." so sadly
It made his mother cry.

At night he played his zither,
By day worked in the mine.
His friend was Hans; together
The boys walked by the Rhine.

"Each day we're growing older,"
Hans said, "This is no life.
I wish I were a soldier!"
And snapped his pocketknife.

War came, and Hans was taken,
But Heinrich did not fight.
"Ich wünscht', ich wäre ein Vöglein,"
Sang Heinrich every night.

"Dear Heinrich," said the letter,
"I hope this finds you fine.
The war could not be better,
It's women, song and wine."

A letter came for Heinrich,
The same that he'd sent East
To Hans, his own handwriting
Returned, and marked *Deceased*.

*

"You'll never be a beauty,"
The doctor said, "You scamp!
We'll give you special duty —
A concentration camp."

And now the truck was nearing
The place. They passed a house;
A radio was blaring
The *Weiner Blut* of Strauss.

The banks were bright with flowers,
The birds sang in the wood;
There was a fence with towers
On which armed sentries stood.

They stopped. The men dismounted;
Heinrich got down—at last!
"That chimney," said the sergeant,
"That's where the Jews are gassed."

*

Each day he sorted clothing,
Skirt, trousers, boot and shoe,
Till he was filled with loathing
For every size of Jew.

"Come in! What is it, Private?"
"Please Sir, that vacancy . . .
I wonder, could I have it?"
"Your papers! Let me see . . .

"You're steady and you're sober . . .
But have you learned to kill?"
Said Heinrich, "No, *Herr Ober-
Leutnant,* but I will!"

"The Reich can use your spirit.
Report to Unit Four.
Here is an arm-band—wear it!
Dismissed! Don't slam the door."

*

"Ich wünscht', ich wäre ein Vöglein,"
Sang Heinrich, "I would fly ..."
They knew that when they heard him
The next day they would die.

They stood in silence praying
At midnight when they heard
The zither softly playing,
The singing of the Bird.

He stared into the fire,
He sipped a glass of wine.
"Ich wünscht'," his voice rose higher,
Ich wäre ein Vöglein ..."

A dog howled in its kennel,
He thought of Hans and cried.
The stars looked down from heaven.
That day the children died.

*

"The Russian tanks are coming!"
The wind bore from the east
A cannonade, a drumming
Of small arms that increased.

Heinrich went to Headquarters.
He found the Colonel dead
With pictures of his daughters,
A pistol by his head.

He thought, his courage sinking,
"There's always the SS ..."
He found the Major drinking
In a woman's party dress.

The prisoners were shaking
Their barracks. Heinrich heard
A sound of timber breaking,
A shout, "Where is the Bird?"

*

The Russian was completing
A seven-page report.
He wrote: "We still are beating
The woods . . ." then he stopped short.

A little bird was flitting
Outside, from tree to tree.
He turned where he was sitting
And watched it thoughtfully.

He pulled himself together,
And wrote: "We've left no stone
Unturned—but not a feather!
It seems the Bird has flown.

"Description? Half a dozen
Group snapshots, badly blurred;
And which is Emma's cousin
God knows, and which the Bird!

"He could be in the Western
Or in the Eastern Zone.
I'd welcome a suggestion
If anything is known."

*

Ich wünscht', ich wäre ein Vöglein,"
Sings Heinrich, "I would fly
Across the sea," so sadly
It makes his children cry.

THE SILENT GENERATION

When Hitler was the Devil
He did as he had sworn
With such enthusiasm
That even, *donnerwetter,*
The Germans say, "Far better
Had he been never born!"

It was my generation
That put the Devil down
With great enthusiasm.
But now our occupation
Is gone. Our education
Is wasted on the town.

We lack enthusiasm.
Life seems a mystery;
It's like the play a lady
Told me about: "It's not . . .
It doesn't *have* a plot,"
She said, "it's history."

A STORY ABOUT CHICKEN SOUP

In my grandmother's house there was always chicken soup
And talk of the old country—mud and boards,
Poverty,
The snow falling down the necks of lovers.

Now and then, out of her savings
She sent them a dowry. Imagine
The rice-powdered faces!
And the smell of the bride, like chicken soup.

But the Germans killed them.
I know it's in bad taste to say it,
But it's true. The Germans killed them all.

       *

In the ruins of Berchtesgaden
A child with yellow hair
Ran out of a doorway.

A German girl-child—
Cuckoo, all skin and bones—
Not even enough to make chicken soup.
She sat by the stream and smiled.

Then as we splashed in the sun
She laughed at us.
We had killed her mechanical brothers,
So we forgave her.

       *

The sun is shining.
The shadows of the lovers have disappeared.
They are all eyes; they have some demand on me—
They want me to be more serious than I want to be.

They want me to stick in their mudhole
Where no one is elegant.
They want me to wear old clothes,
They want me to be poor, to sleep in a room with many others—

Not to walk in the painted sunshine
To a summer house,
But to live in the tragic world forever.

A BOWER OF ROSES

The mixture of smells—
of Algerian tobacco,
wine barrels, and urine—
I'll never forget it,
he thought, if I live to be a hundred.

And the whores in every street,
and like flies in the bars . . .
Some of them looked familiar:
there was a Simone Simone,
a Veronica.

And some were original,
like the two who stood on a corner,
a brunette with hair like ink
and a platinum blonde,
holding a Great Dane on a leash.

"A monster," said Margot.
"Those three give me the shivers."

The other girls were of the same opinion.
One said, "And, after all,
think what a dog like that must cost to feed."

This was conclusive. They stared out at the street—
there was nothing more to be said.

                    *

When they gave him a pass at the hospital
he would make for the bar in Rue Sainte Apolline
Margot frequented. Sitting in a corner
as though she had been waiting . . .

Like the sweetheart on a postcard
gazing from a bower of roses . . .
"Je t'attends toujours."

For ten thousand francs
she would let him stay the night,
and a thousand for the concièrge.
The maid, too, must have something.

Then, finally, he would be alone with her.
Her face a perfect oval,
a slender neck, brown hair ...

It surprised him that a girl
who looked delicate in her clothes
was voluptuous when she stood naked.

*

He caught up with the division in Germany,
at Dusseldorf, living in houses
a hundred yards from the Rhine.

Now and then a shell flew over.
For every shell Krupp fired
General Motors sent back four.

Division found some cases of beer,
and cigars, and passed them around—
a taste of the luxury
that was coming. The post-war.

One morning they crossed the Rhine.
Then they were marching through villages
where the people stood and stared.
Then they rode in convoys of trucks
on the autobahns. Deeper in.

The areas on the map of Germany
marked with the swastika kept diminishing,
and then, one day, there were none left.

*

They were ordered back to France,
only sixty kilometers from Paris.

Once more he found himself climbing the stairs.
He knocked, and heard footsteps.
"Who is it?"
          The door opened a crack,
then wide, and he was holding her.
"My God," she said, "chéri,
I never thought to see you again."

That night, lying next to her,
he thought about young women
he had known back in the States
who would not let you do anything.
And a song of the first war . . .
"How Are You Going to Keep Them Down on the Farm?
(After They've Seen Paree)."

He supposed this was what life taught you,
that words you thought were a joke,
and applied to someone else,
were real, and applied to you.

ON THE LAWN AT THE VILLA

On the lawn at the villa—
That's the way to start, eh, reader?
We know where we stand—somewhere expensive—
You and I *imperturbes,* as Walt would say,
Before the diversions of wealth, you and I *engagés.*

On the lawn at the villa
Sat a manufacturer of explosives,
His wife from Paris,
And a young man named Bruno,

And myself, being American,
Willing to talk to these malefactors,
The manufacturer of explosives, and so on,
But somehow superior. By that I mean democratic.
It's complicated, being an American,
Having the money and the bad conscience, both at the same time.
Perhaps, after all, this is not the right subject for a poem.

We were all sitting there paralyzed
In the hot Tuscan afternoon,
And the bodies of the machine-gun crew were draped over
    the balcony.
So we sat there all afternoon.

ON THE LEDGE

I can see the coast coming near . . .
one of our planes, a Thunderbolt, plunging down
and up again. Seconds later
we heard the rattle of machine guns.

That night we lay among hedgerows.
The night was black. There was thrashing
in a hedgerow, a burst of firing . . .
in the morning, a dead cow.

A plane droned overhead . . .
one of theirs,
diesel, with a rhythmic sound.
Then the bombs came whistling down.

                    *

We were strung out on an embankment
side by side in a straight line,
like infantry in World War One
waiting for the whistle to blow.

The Germans knew we were there
and were firing everything they had,
bullets passing right above.
I knew that in a moment the order would come.

There is a page in Dostoevsky
about a man being given the choice
to die, or to stand on a ledge
through all eternity . . .

alive and breathing the air,
looking at the trees, and sky . . .
the wings of a butterfly
as it drifts from stem to stem.

But men who have stepped off the ledge
know all that there is to know:
who survived the Bloody Angle,
Verdun, the first day on the Somme.

As it turned out, we didn't have to.
Instead, they used Typhoons.
They flew over our heads, firing rockets
on the German positions.

So it was easy. We just strolled
over the embankment,
and down the other side,
and across an open field.

Yet, like the man on the ledge,
I still haven't moved ...
watching an ant
climb a blade of grass and climb back down.

III

A DISCOVERY OF AMERICA

TO THE WESTERN WORLD

A siren sang, and Europe turned away
From the high castle and the shepherd's crook.
Three caravels went sailing to Cathay
On the strange ocean, and the captains shook
Their banners out across the Mexique Bay.

And in our early days we did the same.
Remembering our fathers in their wreck
We crossed the sea from Palos where they came
And saw, enormous to the little deck,
A shore in silence waiting for a name.

The treasures of Cathay were never found.
In this America, this wilderness
Where the axe echoes with a lonely sound,
The generations labor to possess
And grave by grave we civilize the ground.

WEST

On US 101
I felt the traffic running like a beast,
Roaring in space.
                   Tamalpais
The red princess slopes
In honeyed burial from hair to feet;
The sharp lifting fog
Uncurtains Richmond and the ridge
—With two red rubies set upon the bridge—
And curtains them again.

Ranching in Bolinas, that's the life,
If you call cattle life.
To sit on a veranda with a glass
And see the sprinklers watering your land
And hear the peaches dropping from the trees
And hear the ocean in the redwood trees,

The whales of time,
Masts of the long voyages of earth,
In whose tall branches day
Hangs like a Christmas toy.

On their red columns drowse
The eagles battered at the Western gate;
These trees have held the eagles in their state
When Rome was still a rumor in the boughs.

HOT NIGHT ON WATER STREET

A hot midsummer night on Water Street—
The boys in jeans were combing their blond hair,
Watching the girls go by on tired feet;
And an old woman with a witch's stare
Cried "Praise the Lord!" She vanished on a bus
With hissing air brakes, like an incubus.

Three hardware stores, a barbershop, a bar,
A movie playing Westerns—where I went
To see a dream of horses called *The Star*...
Some day, when this uncertain continent
Is marble, and men ask what was the good
We lived by, dust may whisper "Hollywood."

Then back along the river bank on foot
By moonlight.... On the West Virginia side
An owlish train began to huff and hoot;
It seemed to know of something that had died.
I didn't linger—sometimes when I travel
I think I'm being followed by the Devil.

At the newsstand in the lobby, a cigar
Was talkative: "Since I've been in this town
I've seen one likely woman, and a car
As she was crossing Main Street knocked her down."
I was a stranger here myself, I said,
And bought the *New York Times*, and went to bed.

THERE IS

1

Look! From my window there's a view
of city streets
where only lives as dry as tortoises
can crawl—the Galapagos of desire.

There is the day of Negroes with red hair
and the day of insane women on the subway;
there is the day of the word Trieste
and the night of the blind man with the electric guitar.

But I have no profession. Like a spy
I read the papers—Situations Wanted.
Surely there is a secret
which, if I knew it, would change everything!

2

I have the poor man's nerve-tic, irony.
I see through the illusions of the age!
The bell tolls, and the hearse advances,
and the mourners follow, for my entertainment.

I tread the burning pavement,
the streets where drunkards stretch
like photographs of civil death
and trumpets strangle in electric shelves.

The mannequins stare at me scornfully.
I know they are pretending
all day to be in earnest.
And can it be that love is an illusion?

When darkness falls on the enormous street
the air is filled with Eros, whispering.
Eyes, mouths, contrive to meet
in silence, fearing they may be prevented.

3

O businessmen like ruins,
bankers who are Bastilles,
widows, sadder than the shores of lakes,
then you were happy, when you still could tremble!

But all night long my window
sheds tears of light.
I seek the word. The word is not forthcoming.
O syllables of light ... O dark cathedral...

WALT WHITMAN AT BEAR MOUNTAIN

> *"... life which does not give the preference to*
> *any other life, of any previous period, which*
> *therefore prefers its own existence ...*
> *—Ortega y Gasset*

Neither on horseback nor seated,
But like himself, squarely on two feet,
The poet of death and lilacs
Loafs by the footpath. Even the bronze looks alive
Where it is folded like cloth. And he seems friendly.

"Where is the Mississippi panorama
And the girl who played the piano?
Where are you, Walt?
The Open Road goes to the used-car lot.

"Where is the nation you promised?
These houses built of wood sustain
Colossal snows,
And the light above the street is sick to death.

"As for the people—see how they neglect you!
Only a poet pauses to read the inscription."

"I am here," he answered.
"It seems you have found me out.
Yet, did I not warn you that it was Myself
I advertised? Were my words not sufficiently plain?

"I gave no prescriptions,
And those who have taken my moods for prophecies
Mistake the matter."
Then, vastly amused—"Why do you reproach me?
I freely confess I am wholly disreputable.
Yet I am happy, because you have found me out."

A crocodile in wrinkled metal loafing ...

Then all the realtors,
Pickpockets, salesmen, and the actors performing
Official scenarios,
Turned a deaf ear, for they had contracted
American dreams.

But the man who keeps a store on a lonely road,
And the housewife who knows she's dumb,
And the earth, are relieved.

All that grave weight of America
Cancelled! Like Greece and Rome.
The future in ruins!
The castles, the prisons, the cathedrals
Unbuilding, and roses
Blossoming from the stones that are not there ...

The clouds are lifting from the high Sierras,
The Bay mists clearing.
And the angel in the gate, the flowering plum,
Dances like Italy, imagining red.

THE REDWOODS

Mountains are moving, rivers
are hurrying. But we
are still.

We have the thoughts of giants—
clouds, and at night the stars.

And we have names—guttural, grotesque—
Hamet, Og—names with no syllables.

And perish, one by one, our roots
gnawed by the mice. And fall.

And are too slow for death, and change
to stone. Or else too quick,

like candles in a fire. Giants
are lonely. We have waited long

for someone. By our waiting, surely
there must be someone at whose touch

our boughs would bend; and hands
to gather us; a spirit

to whom we are light as the hawthorn tree.
O if there is a poet

let him come now! We stand at the Pacific
like great unmarried girls,

turning in our heads the stars and clouds,
considering whom to please.

INDIAN COUNTRY

1. *The Shadow-hunter*

This prairie light . . . I see
a warrior and a child.

The man points, and the child
runs after a butterfly.

Rising and floating in the windy field,
that's how they learned to run . . .

Plenty Coups,
Red Cloud, Coyote, Pine Marten.

Now I will lie down in the grass
that Plenty Coups loved.

There are voices in the wind, strong voices
in the tenderness of these leaves,

and the deer move with the shade
into the hills I dream of.

There the young men live by hunting
the shadows of ideas,

and at night they march no further.
Their tents shine in the moonlight.

2. *Black Kettle Raises the Stars and Stripes*

"Nits make lice," said Chivington.
"Kill the nits and you'll get no lice."

The white men burst in at sunrise, shooting and stabbing.
And there was old Black Kettle
tying the Stars and Stripes to his tent pole,
and the squaws running in every direction

around Sand Creek,
a swept corner of the American consciousness.

And it's no use playing the tuba to a dead Indian.

3. *On the Prairie*

The wind in the leaves makes a sound
like clear running water.

I can smell the store where harness used to be sold. . . .
Morning of little leaves,

morning of cool, clear sunlight,
when the house stirred with the earnestness

of the life they really had . . .
morning with a clang of machinery.

Now an old man sits on the porch;
I can hear it every time he clears his throat . . .

as I stand here, holding the jack,
in the middle of my generation,

by the Lethe of asphalt and dust
and human blood spilled carelessly.

When I look back I see
a field full of grasshoppers.

The hills are hidden with a cloud.
And what pale king sits in the glass?

THE CLIMATE OF PARADISE

A story about Indians,
the tribe that claimed Mt. Shasta ...

Five lawyers said, "It's ridiculous!
What possible use can they have for the mountain?"

The interpreter said, "Your Honor,
they say that their gods live there."

*

How different this is from the Buzzy Schofields,
people I met in Pasadena.

Green lawns, imposing villas—
actually, these are caves inhabited

by Pufendorf's dwarfs and Vico's
Big Feet, the "abandoned by God."

Thought, says Vico, begins in caves—
but not the Buzzy Schofields'.

They're haunted by Red China—
bugles—a sky lit with artillery.

They're terrified they'll be brainwashed.
They can see themselves breaking under torture ...

"Stop! I'm on your side!
You're making a terrible mistake!"

O even in Paradise
the mind would make its own winter.

IN CALIFORNIA

Here I am, troubling the dream coast
With my New York face,
Bearing among the realtors
And tennis-players my dark preoccupation.

There once was an epical clatter—
Voices and banjos, Tennessee, Ohio,
Rising like incense in the sight of heaven.
Today, there is an angel in the gate.

Lie back, Walt Whitman,
There, on the fabulous raft with the King and the Duke!
For the white row of the Marina
Faces the Rock. Turn round the wagons here.

Lie back! We cannot bear
The stars any more, those infinite spaces.
Let the realtors divide the mountain,
For they have already subdivided the valley.

Rectangular city blocks astonished
Herodotus in Babylon,
Cortez in Tenochtitlan,
And here's the same old city-planner, death.

We cannot turn or stay.
For though we sleep, and let the reins fall slack,
The great cloud-wagons move
Outward still, dreaming of a Pacific.

IN THE SUBURBS

There's no way out.
You were born to waste your life.
You were born to this middleclass life

As others before you
Were born to walk in procession
To the temple, singing.

THE INNER PART

When they had won the war
And for the first time in history
Americans were the most important people—

When the leading citizens no longer lived in their shirt sleeves,
And their wives did not scratch in public;
Just when they'd stopped saying "Gosh!"—

When their daughters seemed as sensitive
As the tip of a fly rod,
And their sons were as smooth as a V-8 engine—

Priests, examining the entrails of birds,
Found the heart misplaced, and seeds
As black as death, emitting a strange odor.

LINES WRITTEN NEAR SAN FRANCISCO

1

I wake and feel the city trembling.
Yes, there is something unsettled in the air
And the earth is uncertain.

And so it was for the tenor Caruso.
He couldn't sleep—you know how the ovation
Rings in your ears, and you re-sing your part.

And then the ceiling trembled
And the floor moved. He ran into the street.
Never had Naples given him such a reception!

The air was darker than Vesuvius.
"*O mamma mia,*"
He cried, "I've lost my voice!"

At that moment the hideous voice of Culture,
Hysterical woman, thrashing her arms and legs,
Shrieked from the ruins.

At that moment everyone became a performer.
Otello and Don Giovanni
And Figaro strode on the midmost stage.

In the high window of a burning castle
Lucia raved. Black horses
Plunged through fire, dragging the wild bells.

The curtains were wrapped in smoke. Tin swords
Were melting; masks and ruffs
Burned—and the costumes of the peasants' chorus.

Night fell. The white moon rose
And sank in the Pacific. The tremors
Passed under the waves. And Death rested.

Now, as we stand idle,
Watching the silent, bowler-hatted man,
The engineer, who writes in the smoking field;

Now as he hands the paper to a boy,
Who takes it and runs to a group of waiting men,
And they disperse and move toward their wagons,

Mules bray and the wagons move—
Wait! Before you start
(Already the wheels are rattling on the stones)

Say, did your fathers cross the dry Sierras
To build another London?
Do Americans always have to be second-rate?

Wait! For there are spirits
In the earth itself, or the air, or sea.
Where are the aboriginal American devils?

Cloud shadows, pine shadows
Falling across the bright Pacific bay . . .
(Already they have nailed rough boards together)

Wait only for the wind
That rustles in the eucalyptus tree.
Wait only for the light

That trembles on the petals of a rose.
(The mortar sets—banks are the first to stand)
Wait for a rose, and you may wait forever.

The silent man mops his head and drinks
Cold lemonade. "San Francisco
Is a city second only to Paris."

3

Every night, at the end of America
We taste our wine, looking at the Pacific.
How sad it is, the end of America!

While we were waiting for the land
They'd finished it—with gas drums
On the hilltops, cheap housing in the valleys

Where lives are mean and wretched.
But the banks thrive and the realtors
Rejoice—they have their America.

Still, there is something unsettled in the air.
Out there on the Pacific
There's no America but the Marines.

Whitman was wrong about the People,
But right about himself. The land is within.
At the end of the open road we come to ourselves.

Though mad Columbus follows the sun
Into the sea, we cannot follow.
We must remain, to serve the returning sun,

And to set tables for death.
For we are the colonists of Death—
Not, as some think, of the English.

And we are preparing thrones for him to sit,
Poems to read, and beds
In which it may please him to rest.

This is the land
The pioneers looked for, shading their eyes
Against the sun—a murmur of serious life.

OUTWARD

The staff slips from the hand
Hissing and swims on the polished floor.
It glides away to the desert.

It floats like a bird or lily
On the waves, to the ones who are arriving.
And if no god arrives,

Then everything yearns outward.
The honeycomb cell brims over
And the atom is broken in light.

Machines have made their god. They walk or fly.
The towers bend like Magi, mountains weep,
Needles go mad, and metal sheds a tear.

*

The astronaut is lifted
Away from the world, and drifts.
How easy it is to be there!

How easy to be anyone, anything but oneself!
The metal of the plane is breathing;
Sinuously it swims through the stars.

ON THE EVE

There is something sad about property
where it ends, in California.

A patch of white moving in a crack of the fence ...
It is the rich widow—
when the dogs howl, she howls like a dog.

                *

At night in San Francisco
the businessmen and drunkards
sink down to the ocean floor.

Their lives are passing.
There is nothing in those depths
but the teeth of sharks and the earbones of whales.

Their lives are passing
slowly under the scrutiny
of goggle eyes, in waves that are vaguely

connected to women.
The women stand up in cages
and do it, their breasts in yellow light.

The businessmen of San Francisco
are mildly exhilarated.
Lifting their heavy arms and feet

they stamp on the ocean floor.
They rise from the ooze of the ocean floor
to the lights that float on the surface.

                *

It is like night in St. Petersburg.
From the Bay a foghorn sounds,

and ships, wrapped in a mist,
creep out with their heavy secrets
to the war "that no one wants."

77

LOVE, MY MACHINE

Love, my machine,
We rise by this escape,
We travel on the shocks we make.

For every man and woman
Is an immortal spirit
Trapped and dazed on a star shoot.

Tokyo, come in!
Yuzuru Karagiri, do you read me?
San Francisco, darkest of cities, do you read me?

Here is eternal space,
Here is eternal solitude.
Is it any different with you on earth?

There are so many here!
Here's Gandhi, here's Jesus,
Moses, and all the other practical people.

By the light of the stars
This night is serious.
I am going into the night to find a world of my own.

AMERICAN DREAMS

In dreams my life came toward me,
my loves that were slender as gazelles.
But America also dreams. . . .
Dream, you are flying over Russia,
dream, you are falling in Asia.

As I look down the street
on a typical sunny day in California
it is my house that is burning
and my dear ones that lie in the gutter
as the American army enters.

Every day I wake far away
from my life, in a foreign country.
These people are speaking a strange language.
It is strange to me
and strange, I think, even to themselves.

THE STREET

Here comes the subway grating fisher
letting down his line through the sidewalk.

Yesterday there was the running man
who sobbed and wept as he ran.

Today there is the subway grating fisher.
Standing as if in thought. . . .

He fishes a while. Then winds up the line
and continues to walk, looking down.

AMERICAN CLASSIC

It's a classic American scene—
a car stopped off the road
and a man trying to repair it.

The woman who stays in the car
in the classic American scene
stares back at the freeway traffic.

They look surprised, and ashamed
to be so helpless ...
let down in the middle of the road!

To think that their car would do this!
They look like mountain people
whose son has gone against the law.

But every night they set out food
and the robber goes skulking back to the trees.
That's how it is with the car ...

it's theirs, they're stuck with it.
Now they know what it's like to sit
and see the world go whizzing by.

In the fume of carbon monoxide and dust
they are not such good Americans
as they thought they were.

The feeling of being left out
through no fault of your own, is common.
That's why I say, an American classic.

LITTLE COLORED FLAGS

Lines of little colored flags
advertising Foreign Motor Sales ...
Mario's, the beauty salon,
the hardware store with its display
of wheelbarrows and garbage cans ...

Most people here are content
to make a decent living.
They take pride in their homes and raising a family.
The women attend meetings of the P.T.A.
Sometimes they drive in to New York
for a day's shopping and the theater.
Their husbands belong to the golf club
or the yacht club.
It makes sense to own a boat if you live in the area.

They go on vacation to Bermuda,
or Europe. Even the Far East.

There aren't too many alternatives.
The couple sitting in the car
will either decide to go home
or to a motel.
Afterwards, they may continue
to see each other, in which case
there will probably be a divorce,
or else they may decide
to stop seeing each other.

Another favorite occupation is gardening ...
wind rushing in the leaves like a sea.
And the sea itself is there
behind the last house at the end of the street.

THE BEADED PEAR

Kennst du das Land, wo die Zitronen blüh'n?
Goethe, *"Mignon"*

1 *Shopping*

Dad in Bermuda shorts, Mom her hair in curlers,
Jimmy, sixteen, and Darlene who is twelve,
are walking through the Smith Haven Mall.

Jimmy needs a new pair of shoes.
In the Mall by actual count
there are twenty-two stores selling shoes:
Wise Shoes, Regal Shoes,
National Shoes, Naturalizer Shoes,
Stride Rite, Selby, Hanover ...

Dad has to buy a new lock for the garage,
Mom and Darlene want to look at clothes.
They agree to meet again in an hour
at the fountain.

The Mall is laid out like a cathedral
with two arcades that cross—
Macy's at one end of the main arcade,
Abraham and Straus at the other.
At the junction of transept and nave
there is a circular, sunken area
with stairs where people sit,
mostly teenagers, smoking
and making dates to meet later.
This is what is meant by "at the fountain."

2 *"Why don't you get transferred, Dad?"*

One of Jimmy's friends comes by in his car,
and Jimmy goes out. "Be careful,"
Mom says. He has to learn to drive,
but it makes her nervous thinking about it.

Darlene goes over to see Marion
whose father is being transferred
to a new branch of the company
in Houston. "Why don't you get transferred, Dad?"

"I'd like to," he replies.
"I'd also like a million dollars."

This is a constant topic in the family:
where else you would like to live.
Darlene likes California—
"It has beautiful scenery
and you get to meet all the stars."
Mom prefers Arizona, because of a picture
she saw once, in *Good Housekeeping.*
Jimmy doesn't care,
and Dad likes it here. "You can find anything
you want right where you are."
He reminds them of *The Wizard of Oz,*
about happiness, how it is found
right in your own backyard.

Dad's right, Mom always says.
The Wizard of Oz is a tradition
in the family. They see it every year.

3 *The Beaded Pear*

The children are home at six,
and they sit down to eat. Mom insists
on their eating together at least once
every week. It keeps the family together.

After helping with the dishes
the children go out again,
and Mom and Dad settle down to watch
"Hollywood Star Time," with Bobby Darin,
Buddy Rich, Laura Nyro,
Judy Collins, and Stevie Wonder.

When this is over he looks in *TV Guide,*
trying to decide
whether to watch "Salty O'Rourke (1945).
A gambler who is readying his horse
for an important race
falls in love with a pretty teacher,"
or, "Delightful family fare,
excellent melodrama of the Mafia."

She has seen enough television
for one night. She gets out the beaded pear
she bought today in the Mall.

A "Special $1.88 do-it-yourself Beaded Pear.
No glueing or sewing required.
Beautiful beaded fruit is easily assembled
using enclosed pins, beads, and decorative material."

She says, "It's not going to be so easy."

"No," he says, "it never is."

She speaks again. "There is a complete series.
Apple, Pear, Banana, Lemon, Orange,
Grapes, Strawberry, Plum, and Lime."

BACK IN THE STATES

It was cold, and all they gave him to wear
was a shirt. And he had malaria.

There was continual singing of hymns—
"Nearer My God to Thee" was a favorite.
And a sound like running water . . .
it took him a while to figure it.

Weeping, coming from the cells
of the men who had been condemned.

Now here he was, back in the States,
idly picking up a magazine,
glancing through the table of contents.

Already becoming like the rest of us.

IV

MODERN LIVES

THE BOARDER

The time is after dinner. Cigarettes
        Glow on the lawn;
Glasses begin to tinkle; TV sets
        Have been turned on.

The moon is brimming like a glass of beer
        Above the town,
And love keeps her appointments — "Harry's here!"
        "I'll be right down."

But the pale stranger in the furnished room
        Lies on his back
Looking at paper roses, how they bloom,
        And ceilings crack.

SUMMER MORNING

There are whole blocks in New York
Where no one lives —
A district of small factories.
And there's a hotel; one morning

When I was there with a girl
We saw in the window opposite
Men and women working at their machines.
Now and then one looked up.

Toys, hardware — whatever they made,
It's been worn out.
I'm fifteen years older myself —
Bad years and good.

So I have spoiled my chances.
For what? Sheer laziness,
The thrill of an assignation,
My life that I hold in secret.

NEWSPAPER NIGHTS

After midnight when the presses were rolling
we would leave the *Herald Tribune* building
and walk up to Times Square.
The three of us would still be laughing and joking.

I can see a sign that says Schenley.
There are numbers high on a building
telling the time, 12:27,
the temperature, 36.

We have the streets all to ourselves.
There is only the sound of an ambulance or a fire.
There are only the lights that still keep changing
from green to red and back to green in silence.

AFTER MIDNIGHT

The dark streets are deserted,
With only a drugstore glowing
Softly, like a sleeping body;

With one white, naked bulb
In the back, that shines
On suicides and abortions.

Who lives in these dark houses?
I am suddenly aware
I might live here myself.

The garage man returns
And puts the change in my hand,
Counting the singles carefully.

SIMPLICITY

Climbing the staircase
step by step, feeling my way . . .
I seem to have some trouble with my vision.
The stairs are littered with paper,
eggshells, and other garbage.
Then she comes to the door.
Without eye-shadow or lipstick,
with her hair tied in a bun,
in a white dress, she seem ethereal.

"Peter," she says, "how nice!
I thought that you were Albert,
but he hardly ever comes."

She says, "I hope you like my dress.
It's simple. I made it myself.
Nowadays everyone's wearing simple things.
The thing is to be sincere,
and then, when you're tired of something,
you just throw it away."

I'll spare you the description
of all her simple objects:
the bed pushed in one corner;
the naked bulb that hangs
on a wire down from the ceiling
that is stamped out of metal
in squares, each square containing
a pattern of leaves and flowers;
the window with no blinds, admitting
daylight, and the wall
where a stream of yellow ice hangs down
in waves.

    She is saying
"I have sat in this room
all day. There is a time
when you just stare at the wall
all day, and nothing moves.

I can't go on like this any longer,
counting the cracks in the wall,
doting on my buttons."

I seem to be disconnected
from the voice that is speaking
and the sound of the voice that answers.
Things seem to be moving into a vacuum.
I put my head in my hands
and try to concentrate.
But the light shines through my hands,

and then (how shall I put it
exactly?) it's as though she begins
giving off vibrations,
waves of resentment, an aura
of hate you could cut with a knife....
Squirming, looking over her shoulder ...
Her whole body seems
to shrink, and she speaks in hisses:

"They want to remove my personality.
They're giving me psychotherapy
and *ikebana*, the art of flower-arrangement.
Some day, I suppose, I'll be cured,
and then I'll go and live in the suburbs,
doting on dogs and small children."

I go down the stairs, feeling my way
step by step. When I come out,
the light on the snow is blinding.
My shoes crunch on ice and my head
goes floating along, and a voice
from a high, barred window cries
"Write me a poem!"

VANDERGAST AND THE GIRL

Vandergast to his neighbors—
the grinding of a garage door
and hiss of gravel in the driveway.

He worked for the insurance company
whose talisman is a phoenix
rising in flames ... *non omnis moriar*.
From his desk he had a view of the street—

translucent raincoats, and umbrellas,
fluorescent plate-glass windows.
A girl knelt down, arranging
underwear on a female dummy—

sea waves and, on the gale,
Venus, these busy days,
poised in her garter-belt and stockings.

                    *

The next day he saw her eating
in the restaurant where he usually ate.

Soon they were having lunch together
elsewhere.

          She came from Dallas.
This was only a start, she was ambitious,
twenty-five and still unmarried.
Green eyes with silver spiricles ...
red hair....

          When he held the car door open
her legs were smooth and slender.

"I was wondering,"
she said, "when you'd get round to it,"
and laughed.

          *

Vandergast says he never intended
having an affair.

                     And was that what this was?
The names that people give to things. . . .
What do definitions and divorce-court proceedings
have to do with the breathless reality?

O little lamp at the bedside
with views of Venice and the Bay of Naples,
you understood! *Lactona* toothbrush
and suitcase bought in a hurry,
you were the witnesses of the love
we made in bed together.

Schrafft's Chocolate Cherries, surely you remember
when she said she'd be true forever,

and, watching "Dark Storm," we decided
there is something to be said, after all,
for soap opera, "if it makes people happy."

                *

The Vandergasts are having some trouble
finding a buyer for their house.

When I go for a walk with Tippy
we pass the unweeded tennis court,
the empty garage, windows heavily shuttered.

Mrs. Vandergast took the children
and went back to her family.

And Vandergast moved to New Jersey,
where he works for an insurance company
whose emblem is the Rock of Gibraltar—
the rest of his life laid out
with the child-support and alimony payments.

As for the girl, she vanished.

Was it worth it? Ask Vandergast.
You'd have to be Vandergast, looking through his eyes
at the house across the street, in Orange, New Jersey.
Maybe on wet days umbrellas and raincoats
set his heart thudding.
                    Maybe

he talks to his pillow, and it whispers,
moving red hair.

In any case, he will soon be forty.

THE STEVENSON POSTER

Talking to someone your own age
who has made a million dollars
you realize that time is passing,
and one thing is sure, you'll never make a million.

He had just bought into a cooperative—
the penthouse, with a magnificent view.
He showed it to me from the patio.
Behind us a roar ... the housewarming party ...
the sound poured outward, over the Atlantic.

"Twelve rooms," he had said—
I was impressed.
Especially by one room that had nothing in it
but a tank that glowed deep blue ...
a tropical aquarium
with coral reefs, places to go in and out.

One fish was adhering to the side of the tank—
"He does the sanitation," said my host.
When I thought of my one and a half rooms
with the Salvation Army furniture,
I could have applied for the job myself.

There were paintings by De Kooning and Hans Hofmann.

In the library, next to a certificate
stating that William Francis Heilbrun
had been "pledged to trout release,"
hung a poster of Adlai Stevenson—
the one where he was running for president
with a hole in the sole of his shoe.

*

Bill and Marion owned a house in East Hampton.
They asked me out one Saturday.
The children had just been given a sailboat—
there was great interest and excitement.
Marion would say, "They're too far out,"
and Bill would tell her not to worry.
Then she want back to *Harper's Bazaar*
and her nails. Whenever I think about her
she is wearing dark glasses and reading *Harper's Bazaar*
or *Vogue,* and polishing her nails.

I would have said they were happy,
but the next time I saw Bill Heilbrun
he and Marion were getting a divorce.

Like other apparently happy couples
they had felt they were "missing out on life."
They kept thinking, Is this all?
Nothing seemed to help, not even analysis,
so they decided to separate, to "start a new life."

They had sold the twelve-room apartment.
The day they moved, he sat down with the movers
and they drank two quarts of whiskey.
They put African drums on the stereo
and went stamping around.
They pried the sanitation expert
off the side of the tank, and flushed him down the toilet.
They tore up the poster of Stevenson
and burned it in the fireplace.

Because the moving men wanted to
and he didn't have the heart to refuse.

THE MIDDLEAGED MAN

There is a middleaged man, Tim Flanagan,
whom everyone calls "Fireball."
Every night he does the rocket-match trick.
"Ten, nine, eight. . . ." On zero
p f f t ! It flies through the air.

Walking to the subway with Flanagan. . .
He tells me that he lives out in Queens
on Avenue Street, the end of the line.
That he "makes his home" with his sister
who has recently lost her husband.

What is it to me?
Yet I can't help imagining what it would be like
to be Flanagan. Climbing the stairs
and letting himself in . . .
I can see him eating in the kitchen.

He stays up late watching television.
From time to time he comes to the window.
At this late hour the streets are deserted.
He looks up and down. He looks right at me,
then he steps back out of sight.

*

Sometimes I wake in the middle of the night
and I have a vision of Flanagan.
He is wearing an old pair of glasses
with a wire bent around the ear
and fastened to the frame with tape.

He is reading a novel by Morley Callaghan.
Whenever I wake he is still there . . .
with his glasses. I wish he would get them fixed.
I cannot sleep as long as there is wire
running from his eye to his ear.

100

THE HOUR OF FEELING

Love, now a universal birth,
From heart to heart is stealing,
From earth to man, from man to earth:
—It is the hour of feeling.
—Wordsworth, *"To My Sister"*

A woman speaks:
"I hear you were in San Francisco.
What did they tell you about me?"

She begins to tremble. I can hear the sound
her elbow made, rapping on the wood.
It was something to see and to hear—
not like the words that pass for life,
things you read about in the papers.

People who read a deeper significance
into everything, every whisper . . .
who believe that a knife crossed with a fork
is a signal . . . by the sheer intensity
of their feeling leave an impression.

And with her, tangled in her hair,
came the atmosphere, four walls,
the avenues of the city
at twilight, the lights going on.

When I left I started to walk.
Once I stopped to look at a window
displaying ice skates and skis.
At another with Florsheim shoes . . .

Thanks to the emotion with which she spoke
I can see half of Manhattan,
the canyons and the avenues.

There are signs high in the air
above Times Square and the vicinity:
a sign for Schenley's Whiskey,
for Admiral Television,
and a sign saying Milltag, whatever that means.

I can see over to Brooklyn and Jersey,
and beyond there are meadows,
and mountains and plains.

THE MEXICAN WOMAN

All he needed was fifty cents
to get a job in Union City.

You wouldn't believe it, he
was in Mexico with Black Jack Pershing.

He lived with a Mexican woman.
Then he followed her, and was wise.

"Baby," he said, "you're a two-timer,
I'm wise to you and the lieutenant."

        *

I gave him the fifty cents,
but the old man's tale still haunts me.

I know what it's like to serve
in Mexico with Black Jack Pershing.

And to walk in the dust and heat . . .
for I can see her hurrying

to the clay wall where they meet,
and I shall be wise to her and the lieutenant.

THE PAWNSHOP

The first time I saw a pawnshop
I thought, Sheer insanity.
A revolver lying next to a camera,
violins hanging in the air like hams. . . .

But in fact there was a reason for everything.

So it is with all these lives:
one is stained from painting with oils;
another has a way of arguing
with a finger along his nose, the Misnagid tradition;
a third sits at a desk made of mahogany.

They are all cunningly displayed
to appeal to someone. Each has its place in the universe.

THE MAN SHE LOVED

                    In the dusk
men with sidelocks, wearing hats
and long black coats walked side by side,
hands clasped behind their backs,
talking Yiddish. It was like being in a foreign country.

The members of the family
arrived one by one . . .
his aunts, his uncle, and his mother
talking about her business
in Venezuela. She had moved to a new building
with enough space and an excellent location.

To their simple, affectionate questions
he returned simple answers.
For how could he explain what it meant to be a writer . . .
a world that was entirely different,
and yet it would include the sofa
and the smell of chicken cooking.

Little did they know as they spoke
that one day they would be immortal
in a novel that commanded the sweep
of Tolstoy, a magnificent creation
that would bring within its compass
offices in Manhattan and jungles
of the Amazon. A grasp of psychology
and sense of the passing of time
that can only be compared to,
without exaggerating, Proust.

The path wound through undergrowth.
Palms rose at an angle from the humid plain.
He passed a hut with chickens and goats . . .
an old man who sat with his back to a wall,
not seeing. A woman came out of a door
and stared after him.

                              In the distance
the purple mountains shone, fading
as the heat increased.

"Let me take a look at it,"
said Joey. He took the watch
from Beth, pried open the back,
and laid it on the table before him.
He reached in his jacket
and produced a jeweler's loupe . . .
screwed it into his eye,
and examined the works.
"I can fix it. It only needs an adjustment."

"Are you sure?" said his sister.
"I wouldn't want anything to happen to it.
Jack gave it to me."

The used-car tycoon. But they never married.
"I've got," he said, "a tiger by the tail,"
meaning the used-car business.

Joey stared at her.
"Don't you think I know my business?"

Siblings. Members of the one family,
tied by affection, and doubt . . .
right down to the funeral
when, looking at the face in the box,
you can be sure. "That's real enough."

Spreading her wings at the piano . . .
"The Man I Love." A pleasant voice
but thin.

She traveled to Central America
on the Grace Line, singing with a band.
White boats on a deep blue sea . . .

at night a trail of fireflies.
"Sitting at the Captain's table,"
"Teeing off at the Liguanea Club."

This picture was taken much earlier . . .
three flappers with knee-high skirts.
1921.
They were still living in Delancey Street.

The songs that year were "Say It With Music"
and "If You Would Care For Me."

SWAY

"Swing and sway with Sammy Kaye"

Everyone at Lake Kearney had a nickname:
there was a Bumstead, a Tonto, a Tex,
and, from the slogan of a popular orchestra,
two sisters, Swing and Sway.

Swing jitterbugged, hopping around
on the dance floor, working up a sweat.
Sway was beautiful. My heart went out to her
when she lifted her heavy rack of dishes
and passed through the swinging door.

She was engaged, to an enlisted man
who was stationed at Fort Dix.
He came once or twice on weekends
to see her. I tried talking to him,
but he didn't answer ... out of stupidity
or dislike, I could not tell which.
In real life he was a furniture salesman.
This was the hero on whom she had chosen
to bestow her affections.

I told her of my ambition:
to write novels conveying the excitement
of life ... the main building lit up
like a liner on Saturday night;
the sound of the band ... clarinet,
saxophone, snare drum, piano.
He who would know your heart (America)
must seek it in your songs.

And the contents of your purse ...
among Kleenex, aspirin,
chewing gum wrappers, combs, et cetera.

"Don't stop," she said, "I'm listening.
Here it is!" flourishing her lighter.

*

In the afternoon when the dishes were washed
and tables wiped, we rowed out on the lake.
I read aloud ... *The Duino Elegies,*
while she reclined, one shapely knee up,
trailing a hand in the water.

She had chestnut-colored hair.
Her eyes were changing like the surface
with ripples and the shadows of clouds.

"Beauty," I read to her, "is nothing
but beginning of Terror we're still just able to bear."

*

She came from Jersey, the industrial wasteland
behind which Manhattan suddenly rises.
I could visualize the street where she lived,
and see her muffled against the cold,
in galoshes, trudging to school.
Running about in tennis shoes
all through the summer ...
I could hear the porch swing squeak
and see into the parlor.
It was divided by a curtain or screen....

"That's it," she said, "all but the screen.
There isn't any."

When she or her sister had a boyfriend
their mother used to stay in the parlor,
pretending to sew, and keeping an eye on them
like Fate.

At night she would lie awake
looking at the sky, spangled over.
Her thoughts were as deep and wide as the sky.
As time went by she had a feeling
of missing out ... that everything
was happening somewhere else.

Some of the kids she grew up with
went crazy ... like a car turning over and over.
One of her friends had been beaten
by the police. Some vital fluid
seemed to have gone out of him.
His arms and legs shook. Busted springs.

*

She said, "When you're a famous novelist
will your write about me?"

I promised ... and tried to keep my promise.

Recently, looking for a toolbox,
I came upon some typewritten pages,
all about her. There she is
in a canoe ... a gust of wind
rustling the leaves along the shore.
Playing tennis, running up and down the baseline.
Down by the boathouse, listening to the orchestra
playing "Sleepy Lagoon."

Then the trouble begins. I can never think of anything
to make the characters do.
We are still sitting in the moonlight
while she finishes her cigarette.
Two people go by, talking in low voices.
A car door slams. Driving off ...

"I suppose we ought to go,"
I say.
                    And she says, "Not yet."

A RIVER RUNNING BY

The air was aglimmer, thousands of snowflakes
falling the length of the street.

Five to eight inches, said the radio.
But in the car it was warm;
she had left the engine running
and sat with both hands on the wheel,
her breast and throat like marble
rising from the pool of the dark.

She apologized for the mess:
the litter of junk mail,
an old pair of sneakers,
a suspicious-looking brown paper bag,
and a tennis racket. She had been meaning
to get rid of it. All last summer
she had wondered why her arm hurt,
until a few days ago when she noticed
that the frame was bent.
                              She played tennis
the way she did everything, carelessly.
She hadn't deserved to win,
one woman told her, lacking the right attitude.

                 *

The fallen snow gleamed in the dark
like water. Everything is a flowing,
you have only to flow with it.

If you did, you would live to regret it.
After a while, passion would wear off
and you would still be faced with life,
the same old dull routine.

They would quarrel and make up
regularly. Within a few years
he would grow morose. The trouble with love
is that you have to believe in it.
Like swimming . . . you have to keep it up.

And those who didn't, who remained
on the sofa watching television,
would live to wish that they had.
It was six of one and half a dozen of the other.

"You're serious. What are you thinking?"

That the snow looks like a river.
But there is no river, it is only an idea,
he thought, standing on the edge.

UNFINISHED LIFE

The "villages" begin further out . . .
post office, high school, bank,
built of brick. The state of mind
is Colonial: four white columns
and a watchtower, also white.

Then screens of trees and evergreens
hide the houses, mile on mile.
When the traffic slows to a halt
your eye is attracted to fragments:
a tailpipe, rusted through,
a hubcap, two feet of chain.
Like a battlefield, some great clash of armor . . .

A slice of black rubber
that has crawled out of a crack
and lies on the road like a snake . . .

Not to mention the guardrail
wrenched and twisted out of shape.

You can visualize the accident:
blood seeping in white hair,
turning it cherry-red.

                    *

She said, "I'll be in the garden
if there is anything you need."

He thanked her, and she left,
closing the door silently.
He opened the box and began to read.
Two hours later he was still at it:

"I am sitting with Van Meer,
the old church to our left,
a new 'American' drugstore across the street—
'drugstore publicis' it says repeatedly.

And the Cinema Saint Germain,
showing 'Les Galets d'Etretats' ...
a woman named Virna Lisi with her mouth open.
A sign saying 'Henressy,' and the time
in changing numbers.
A 'Brasserie Lipp.'
A pole, painted white, from which a tricolor hangs.
Rue Bonaparte angling left,
making a flatiron with Rue Rennes.
More signs—'Ted Lapidus,' 'Disques Raoul Vidal.' "

The obsession with names and signs,
Peter thought, could be a sign of senility.
Nevertheless, the writing was good,
especially in the places the public would want to read:
his early days in the Village,
then with Norton-Harjes overseas,
and Paris after the war.

The manuscript came to a stop
with a screech of tires, a crash.

A hubcap went rolling in circles,
ringing as it settled.

                        *

J.B. tapped with a pencil
on the box ... swung in his chair
and gazed out the window
at the helmeted head of Minerva
in bas-relief on the adjacent building
where none but a head editor
could see it, and the pigeons.
Sub specie aeternitatis.

Swung back again.... "We'll take it,
but you'll have to write a conclusion.
Why do you look," he said, "so dismayed?
You did an outstanding job with *Monica.*"

This was a historical romance.
The author, a Southern lady, went insane,
and Peter wrote the missing chapters.

"Couldn't we just end with a note
saying that he left it unfinished?"

"No" said J.B., "I don't think so."
He had the look on his face—inspiration.
There was no arguing with it—
the look he had when he signed the contract
for the cookbook that sold a million.

It was also the look that had turned down
Cards of Identity and *Go Tell It on the Mountain*.

He handed the manuscript over ...
"It needs some final view of things."

Profession of Faith

As a writer I imagine characters,
giving them definite features
and bodies, a color of hair.
I imagine what they feel
and, finally, make them speak.

Increasingly I have come to believe
that the things we imagine
are not amusements, they are real.

There stands my wife, in the garden
gathering lilacs ... reaching up,
pulling a branch toward her,
severing the flower with a knife
decisively, like a surgeon.

If I go away, into another country,
all that will remain is a memory.

Once, on a cold winter's night,
driving on a winding road,
fields covered with snow on my left,
on my right a dark body of water,
I conjured up the figure of a man
standing or floating in mid-air.

The things we see and the things we imagine,
afterwards, when you think about them,
are equally composed of words.

It is the words we use, finally,
that matter, if anything does.

*

The last time I saw Van Meer,
if the reader recalls, we were at the Deux Magots
looking across the street
at a *brasserie* and a drugstore,
with people strolling past:
a man with a moustache, wearing a homburg,
the *Légion d'honneur*
in his buttonhole. His wife
in gray, equally distinguished.
Two students, a boy and girl
with dark, nervous eyes.
An old woman, her feet wrapped in rags,
one of the *clochards*
who sleep beneath the bridges.
And the tourists. This year
these is a swarm of Japanese ...
staring at the people in the café,
the people in the café staring back.
Life, that feeds on the spectacle of itself
to no purpose ...

He said, "We are, you and I,
in eternity. The difference between us
and them is that we know it."

116

Shortly after this he died.
But everything is still there.

The shadow of the word
flitting over the scene,
the street and motionless crowd.

QUIET DESPERATION

At the post office he sees Joe McInnes.
Joe says, "We're having some people over.
It'll be informal. Come as you are."

She is in the middle
of preparing dinner. Tonight
she is trying an experiment;
Hal Burgonyaual—Fish-Potato Casserole.
She has cooked and drained the potatoes
and cut the fish in pieces.
Now she has to "mash potatoes,
add butter and hot milk," et cetera.

He relays Joe's invitation.
"No," she says, "not on your life.
Muriel McInnes is no friend of mine."

It appears that she told Muriel
that the Goldins live above their means,
and Muriel told Mary Goldin.

He listens carefully, to get things right.
The feud between the Andersons and the Kellys
began with Ruth Anderson calling Mike Kelly
a reckless driver. Finally
the Andersons had to sell their house and move.

Social life is no joke.
It can be the only life there is.

                *

In the living room the battle of Iwo Jima
is in progress, watched by his son.
Men are dying on the beach,
pinned down by a machine gun.

The marine carrying the satchel charge
falls. Then Sergeant Stryker

picks up the charge and starts running.

Now you are with the enemy machine gun
firing out of the pillbox
as Stryker comes running,
bullets at his heels kicking up dust.

He makes it to the base of the pillbox,
lights the charge, raises up,
and heaves it through the opening.
The pillbox explodes . . .
the NCO's wave, "Move out!"

And he rises to his feet.
He's seen the movie. Stryker gets killed
just as they're raising the flag.

                    *

A feeling of pressure . . .
There is something that needs to be done
immediately.

              But there is nothing,
only himself. His life is passing,
and afterwards there will be eternity,
silence, and infinite space.

He thinks, "Firewood!",
and goes to the basement,
takes the Swede-saw off the wall,
and goes outside, to the woodpile.

He carries an armful to the sawhorse
and saws the logs into smaller pieces.
In twenty minutes he has a pile of firewood
cut just the right length.
He carries the cut logs into the house
and arranges them in a neat pile
next to the fireplace.

Then looks around for something else to do,
to relieve the feeling of pressure.

The dog!
He will take the dog for a walk.

*

They make a futile procession ...
he commanding her to "Heel!",
she dragging back or straining ahead.

The leaves are turning yellow.
Between the trunks of the trees
the cove is blue, with ripples.
The swans—this year there are seven—
are sailing line astern.

But when you come closer
the rocks above the shore are littered
with daggers of broken glass
where the boys sat on summer nights
and broke beer bottles afterwards.

And the beach is littered, with cans,
containers, heaps of garbage,
newspaper wadded against the sea-wall.
Someone has even dumped a mattress ...
a definite success!
Some daring guy, some Stryker
in the pick-up speeding away.

He cannot bear the sun
going over and going down ...
the trees and houses vanishing
in quiet every day.

120

V

TALES OF VOLHYNIA

DVONYA

In the town of Odessa
there is a garden
and Dvonya is there,
Dvonya whom I love
though I have never been in Odessa.

I love her black hair, and eyes
as green as a salad
that you gather in August
between the roots of alder,
her skin with an odor of wildflowers.

We understand each other perfectly.
We are cousins twice removed.
In the garden we drink our tea,
discussing the plays of Chekhov
as evening falls and the lights begin to twinkle.

But this is only a dream.
I am not there
with my citified speech,
and the old woman is not there
peering between the curtains.

We are only phantoms, bits of ash,
like yesterday's newspaper
or the smoke of chimneys.
All that passed long ago
on a summer night in Odessa.

ADAM YANKEV

Memory rising in the steppes
flows down. On the banks are trees
and towns with golden cupolas.

I can see my mother's family
sitting around the kitchen stove
arguing—the famous Russian theater.

The sisters return—they're breathless,
they've been down to the river—
their arms filled with wildflowers.

                    *

The first clear star comes gliding
over the trees and dark rooftops,
the same world passing here—

voices and shadows of desire,
and the tears of things.... Around us
things want to be understood.

And the moon, so softly gleaming
in furs,
that put a hole through Pushkin.

A SON OF THE ROMANOVS

This is Avram the cello-mender,
the only Jewish sergeant
in the army of the Tsar.
One day he was mending cellos
when they shouted, "The Tsar is coming,
everyone out for inspection!"
When the Tsar saw Avram marching
with Russians who were seven feet tall,
he said, "He must be a genius.
I want that fellow at headquarters."

Luck is given by God.
A wife you must find for yourself.

So Avram married a rich widow
who lived in a house in Odessa.
The place was filled with music ...
Yasnaya Polyana with noodles.

One night in the middle of a concert
they heard a knock at the door.
So Avram went. It was a beggar,
a Russian, who had been blessed
by God—that is, he was crazy.
And he said, "I'm a natural son
of the Grand Duke Nicholas."

And Avram said, "Eat.
I owe your people a favor."
And he said, "My wife is complaining
we need someone to open the door."
So Nicholas stayed with them for years.
Who ever heard of Jewish people
with a footman?

And then the Germans came. Imagine
the scene—the old people
holding on to their baggage,
and the children—they've been told it's a game,
but they don't believe it.
Then the German says, "Who's this?"
pointing at Nicholas,
"he doesn't look like a Jew."
And he said, "I'm the natural son
of the Grand Duke Nicholas."
And they saw he was feeble-minded,
and took him away too, to the death-chamber.

"He could have kept his mouth shut,"
said my Grandmother,
"but what can you expect.
All of those Romanovs were a little bit crazy."

THE COUNTRY HOUSE

You always know what to expect
in a novel by L. V. Kalinin....

"One morning in June, in the provincial town
of X, had you been observant,
you might have seen a stranger
alighting at the railroad station."

From there it moves to a country house,
introduction of the principal characters—
a beautiful girl, a youth
on fire with radical ideas.

There are drawing-room discussions,
picnics at the lake, or a mountain,
if there is one in the vicinity.

Then some misunderstanding—
the young man banished from the house
by the angry father. Tears.

All this with the most meticulous attention
to the "spirit of the times,"
bearing in mind the classical saying,
"Don't be the first to try anything, or the last."

                    *

The tone of his letters was quite different:

"The Polish girl I told you about, who is living with us,
has a wart. Two days ago, the idiot
tried to remove it with lye.
For hours on end the house has been filled with howling,
and I can't think or write."

A NIGHT IN ODESSA

Grandfather puts down his tea-glass
and makes his excuses
and sets off, taking his umbrella.
The street-lamps shine through a fog
and drunkards reel on the pavement.

One man clenches his fists in anger,
another utters terrible sobs. . . .
And women look on calmly.
They like those passionate sounds.
He walks on, grasping his umbrella.

His path lies near the forest.
Suddenly a wolf leaps in the path,
jaws dripping. The man strikes
with the point of his umbrella. . . .
A howl, and the wolf has vanished.

Go on, grandfather, hop!
It takes brains to live here,
not to be beaten and torn
or to lie drunk in a ditch.
Hold on to your umbrella!

He's home. When he opens the door
his wife jumps up to greet him.
Her name is Ninotchka,
she is young and dark and slender,
married only a month or so.

She hurries to get his supper.
But when she puts down the dish
she presses a hand to her side
and he sees that from her hand
red drops of blood are falling.

ISIDOR

Isidor was always plotting
to overthrow the government.
The family lived in one room....
A window rattles,
a woman coughs,
snow drifts over the rooftops ...
despair. An intelligent household.

One day, there's a knock at the door....
The police! A confusion ...
Isidor's wife throws herself
on the mattress ... she groans
as though she is in labor.
The police search everywhere,
and leave. Then a leg comes out ...
an arm ... then a head with spectacles.
Isidor was under the mattress!

When I think about my family
I have a feeling of suffocation.
Next time ... how about the oven?

The mourners are sitting around
weeping and tearing their clothes.
The inspector comes. He looks in the oven ...
there's Isidor, with his eyes
shut fast ... his hands are folded.
The inspector nods, and goes.
Then a leg comes out, and the other.
Isidor leaps, he dances ...

"Praise God, may His Name be exalted!"

A FRIEND OF THE FAMILY

1

Once upon a time in California
the ignorant married the inane
and they lived happily ever after.

But nowadays in the villas
with swimming-pools shaped like a kidney
technicians are beating their wives.
They're accusing each other of mental cruelty.

And the children of those parents
are longing for a rustic community.
They want to get back to the good old days.

Coming toward me . . . a slender
sad girl dressed like a sailor . . .
she says, "Do you have any change?"

One morning when the Mother Superior
was opening another can of furniture polish
Cyd ran for the bus
and came to San Francisco.
Now she drifts from pad to pad. "Hey mister,"
she says, "do you have any change?
I mean, for a hamburger. Really."

2

Let Yevtushenko celebrate the construction
of a hydroelectric dam.
For Russians a dam that works is a miracle.

Why should we celebrate it?
There are lights in the mountain states,
sanatoriums, and the music of Beethoven.

Why should we celebrate the construction
of a better bowling-alley?
Let Yevtushenko celebrate it.

130

A hundred, that's how ancient it is
with us, the rapture of material conquest,
democracy "draining a swamp,
turning the course of a river."

The dynamo howls
but the psyche is still, like an Indian.

And those who are still distending the empire
have vanished beyond our sight.
Far from the sense of hearing
and touch, they are merging
with Asia ...

expanding the war on nature
and the old know-how to Asia.

Nowadays if we want that kind of excitement—
selling beads and whiskey to Indians,
setting up a feed-store,
a market in shoes, tires, machineguns,
material ecstasy, money with hands and feet
stacked up like wooden Indians ...

we must go out to Asia,
or rocketing outward in space.

3
What are they doing in Russia
these nights for entertainment?

In our desert where gaspumps shine
the women are changing their hair—
bubbles of gold and magenta ...
and the young men yearning to be off
full speed ... like Chichikov

in a troika-rocket, plying
the whip, while stars go flying
(Too bad for the off-beat horse!)

131

These nights when a space-rocket rises
and everyone sighs "That's Progress!"
I say to myself "That's Chichikov."

As it is right here on earth—
osteopaths on Mars,
actuaries at the Venus-Hilton ...
Chichikov talking, Chichikov eating,
Chichikov making love.

"Hey Chichikov, where are you going?"

"I'm off to the moon," says Chichikov.

"What will you do when you get there?"

"How do I know?" says Chichikov.

4

Andrei, that fish you caught was my uncle.
He lived in Lutsk, not to confused
with Lodz which is more famous.

When he was twenty he wrote to Chekhov,
and an answer came—"Come to us."
And there it was, signed "Chekhov."

I can see him getting on the train.
It was going to the great city
where Jews had been forbidden.

He went directly to Chekhov's house.
At the door he saw a crowd ...
they told him that Chekhov had just died.

So he went back to his village.
Years passed ... he danced at a wedding
and wept at a funeral. . . .

Then, when Hitler sent for the Jews
he said, "And don't forget Isidor ...
turn left at the pickle-factory."

Andrei, all my life I've been haunted
by Russia—a plain,
a cold wind from the *shtetl*.

I can hear the wheels of the train.
It is going to Radom,
it is going to Jerusalem. . . .

In the night where candles shine
I have a luminous family . . .
people with their arms round each other

forever.

5

I can see myself getting off the train.
"Say, can you tell me how to get . . ."

To Chekhov's house perhaps?

That's what everyone wants, and yet
Chekhov was just a man . . . with ideas,
it's true. As I said to him once,
where on earth do you meet those people?

Vanya who is long-suffering
and Ivanov who is drunk.

And the man, I forget his name,
who thinks everything is forbidden . . .
that you have to have permission
to run, to shout. . . .

And the people who say, "Tell us,
what is it you do exactly to justify your existence?"

These idiots rule the world,
Chekhov knew it, and yet
I think he was happy, on his street.
People live here . . . you'd be amazed.

BARUCH

1

There is an old folk saying:
"He wishes to study the Torah
but he has a wife and family."
Baruch had a sincere love of learning
but he owned a dress-hat factory.

One night he was in his cart returning
to the village. Falling asleep ...
All at once he uttered a cry
and snatched up the reins. He flew!
In the distance there was fire
and smoke. It was the factory,
the factory that he owned was burning.

All night it burned, and by daylight
Lev Baruch was a ruined man.
Some said that it was gypsies,
that sparks from their fire set it burning.
Others said, the workers.

But Lev never murmured. To the contrary,
he said, "It is written,
'by night in a pillar of fire.' "
He said, "Every day of my life
I had looked for a sign in that direction.
Now that I have been relieved of my property
I shall give myself to the Word."

And he did from that day on,
reading Rashi and Maimonides.
He was half way over the *Four Mountains*
when one day, in the midst of his studying,
Lev Baruch fell sick and died.
For in Israel it is also written,
"Prophecy is too great a thing for Baruch."

2

They were lovers of reading in the family.
For instance, Cousin Deborah
who, they said, had read everything ...
The question was, which would she marry,
Tolstoy or Lermontov or Pushkin?

But her family married her off
to a man from Kiev, a timber merchant
who came from Kiev with a team of horses.
On her wedding day she wept,
and at night when they locked her in
she kicked and beat on the door.
She screamed. So much for the wedding!
As soon as it was daylight, Brodsky—
that was his name—drove back to Kiev
like a man pursued, with his horses.

3

We have been devoted to words.
Even here in this rich country
Scripture enters and sits down
and lives with us like a relative.
Taking the best chair in the house ...

His eyes go everywhere, not missing anything.
Wherever his looks go, something ages
and suddenly tears or falls.
Here, a worn place in the carpet,
there, a crack in the wall.

The love of literature goes with us.

On a train approaching midnight
everyone else has climbed into his sarcophagus
except four men playing cards.
There is nothing better than poker—
not for the stakes but the companionship,
trying to outsmart one another.
Taking just one card ...

I am sitting next to the window,
looking at the lights on the prairie
clicking by. From time to time
two or three will come together
then go wandering off again.

Then I see a face, pale and unearthly,
that is flitting along with the train,
passing over the fields and rooftops,
and I hear a voice out of the past:
"He wishes to study the Torah."

WHY DO YOU WRITE ABOUT RUSSIA?

When I was a child
my mother told stories about the country
she came from. Wolves were howling,
snow fell, the drunken Cossack
shouted in the snow.

Rats prowled the floor of the cellar
where the children slept.
Once, after an illness, she was sent
to Odessa, on the sea. There were battleships
painted white, and ladies and gentlemen
walking the esplanade ... white naval uniforms
and parasols.

These stories were told
against a background of tropical night ...
a sea breeze stirring the flowers
that open at dusk, smelling like perfume.
The voice that spoke of freezing cold
itself was warm and infinitely comforting.

So it is with poetry: whatever numbing horrors
it may speak of, the voice itself
tells of love and infinite wonder.

Later, when I came to New York,
I used to go to my grandmother's
in Brooklyn. The names of stations
return in their order like a charm:
Franklin, Nostrand, Kingston.
And members of the family gather:
the three sisters, the one brother,
one of the cousins from Washington,
and myself ... a "student at Columbia."
But what am I really?

For when my grandmother says, "Eat!
People who work with their heads have to eat more. . . ."
Work? Does it deserve a name
so full of seriousness and high purpose?
Gazing across Amsterdam Avenue
at the windows opposite, letting my mind
wander where it will, from the page
to Malaya, or some street in Paris . . .
Drifting smoke. The end will be as fatal
as an opium-eater's dream.

                    *

The view has changed—to evergreens,
a hedge, and my neighbor's roof.
This too is like a dream, the way we live
with our cars and power-mowers . . .
a life that shuns emotion
and the violence that goes with it,
the object being to live quietly
and bring up children to be happy.

Yes, but what are you going to tell them
of what lies ahead?
That the better life seems
the more it goes sour? The child no longer
a child, his happiness all of a sudden
behind him. And he in turn
expected to bring up his children
to be happy . . .

What then do I want?
A life in which there are depths
beyond happiness. As one of my friends,
Grigoryev, says, "Two things
constantly cry out in creation,
the sea and man's soul."

Reaching from where we are
to where we came from ... *Thalassa!*
a view of the sea.

*

I sit listening to the rasp
of a power-saw, the puttering of a motorboat.
The whole meaningless life around me
affirming a positive attitude ...

When a hat appears, a black felt hat,
gliding along the hedge ...
then a long, black overcoat
that falls beneath the knee.

He produces a big, purple handkerchief,
brushes off a chair, and sits.

"It's hot," he says, "but I like to walk,
that way you get to see the world.
And so, what are you reading now?"

Chekhov, I tell him.

"Of course. But have your read Leskov?
There are sentences that will stay in your mind
a whole lifetime.
For instance, in the 'Lady Macbeth,'
when the woman says to her lover,
'You couldn't be nearly as desirous
as you say you are, for I heard you singing' ...
he answers, 'What about gnats?
They sing all their lives, but it's not for joy.'"

So my imaginary friend tells stories
of the same far place the soul comes from.

When I think about Russia
it's not that area of the earth's surface
with Leningrad to the West and Siberia
to the East—I don't know anything
about the continental mass.

It's a sound, such as you hear
in a sea breaking along a shore.

My people came from Russia,
bringing with them nothing
but that sound.

TYPHUS

"The whole earth was covered with snow,
and the Snow Queen's sleigh came gliding.
I heard the bells behind me,
and ran, and ran, till I was out of breath."

During the typhus epidemic
she almost died, and would have
but for the woman who lived next door
who cooked for her and watched by the bed.

When she came back to life
and saw herself in a mirror
they had cut off all her hair.
Also, they had burned her clothing,
and her doll, the only one she ever had,
made out of rags and a stick.

Afterwards, they sent her away
to Odessa, to stay with relatives.
The day she was leaving for home
she bought some plums, as a gift
to take back to the family.
They had never seen such plums!
They were in a window, in a basket.
To buy them she spent her last few kopecks.

The journey took three days by train.
It was hot, and the plums were beginning to spoil.
So she ate them ...
until, finally, all were gone.
The people on the train were astonished.
A child who would eat a plum
and cry ... then eat another!

*

Her sister, Lisa, died of typhus.
The corpse was laid on the floor.

They carried it to the cemetery
in a box, and brought back the box.
"We were poor—a box was worth something."

THE ART OF STORYTELLING

Once upon a time there was a *shocket,*
that is, a kosher butcher,
who went for a walk.

He was standing by the harbor
admiring the ships, all painted white,
when up came three sailors, led by an officer.
"Filth," they said, "who gave you permission?"
and they seized and carried him off.

So he was taken into the navy.
It wasn't a bad life—nothing is.
He learned how to climb and sew,
and to shout "Glad to be of service, Your Excellency!"
He sailed all round the world,
was twice shipwrecked, and had other adventures.
Finally, he made his way back to the village . . .
whereupon he put on his apron, and picked up his knife,
and continued to be a shocket.

At this point, the person telling the story
would say, "This shocket-sailor
was one of our relatives, a distant cousin."

It was always so, they knew they could depend on it.
Even if the story made no sense,
the one in the story would be a relative—
a definite connection with the family.

CHOCOLATES

Once some people were visiting Chekhov.
While they made remarks about his genius
the Master fidgeted. Finally
he said, "Do you like chocolates?"

They were astonished, and silent.
He repeated the question,
whereupon one lady plucked up her courage
and murmured shyly, "Yes."

"Tell me," he said, leaning forward,
light glinting from his spectacles,
"what kind? The light, sweet chocolate
or the dark, bitter kind?"

The conversation became general.
They spoke of cherry centers,
of almonds and Brazil nuts.
Losing their inhibitions
they interrupted one another.
For people may not know what they think
about politics in the Balkans,
or the vexed question of men and women,

but everyone has a definite opinion
about the flavor of shredded coconut.
Finally someone spoke of chocolates filled with liqueur,
and everyone, even the author of *Uncle Vanya,*
was at a loss for words.

As they were leaving he stood by the door
and took their hands.
                    In the coach returning to Petersburg
they agreed that it had been a most
unusual conversation.

144

CAVIARE AT THE FUNERAL

This was the village where the deacon ate all
the caviare at the funeral.
                    Chekhov, *"In the Ravine"*

On the way back from the cemetery
they discussed the funeral arrangements
and the sermon, "such a comfort to the family."

They crowded into the parlor.
It was hot, and voices were beginning to rise.
The deacon found himself beside a plate
heaped with caviare. He helped himself
to a spoonful. Then another.

Suddenly he became aware
that everyone's eyes were upon him,
ruin staring him in the face.
He turned pale. Then tried to carry if off—
one may as well be hanged for a sheep
as a lamb, et cetera.

Meeting their eyes with a stern expression
he took another spoonful,
and another. He finished the plate.

Next morning he was seen at the station
buying a ticket for Kurovskoye,
a village much like ours, only smaller.

VI

ARMIDALE

For George d'Almeida

Il faut voyager loin en aimant sa maison.

AS A MAN WALKS

It's a strange country,
strange for me to have come to.
Cattle standing in a field,
sheep that are motionless
as stones,
the sun sinking in a pile of clouds,
and the eternal flies
getting in your ears and eyes ...

I suppose you become accustomed.
Mrs. Scully was in her kitchen
entertaining two friends
when one said, "Isn't that a snake?"
and pointed. Sure enough
one was sliding around the divider.
She reached for something, the rolling pin,
and stunned it. Then finished it off
with a hammer.

The green-hide and stringy-bark Australian ...
my candidate for survival
in the event of fire, flood,
or nuclear explosion.

As a man walks he creates the road he walks on.
All of my life in America
I must have been reeling out of myself
this red dirt, gravel road.

Three boys seated on motorcycles
conferring ...

                 A little further on,
a beaten-up Holden parked off the road
with two men inside passing the bottle.
Dark-skinned ... maybe they are aboriginal.

I might have been content to live
in Belle Terre, among houses and lawns,
but inside me are gum trees,
and magpies, cackling and whistling,
and a bush-roaming kangaroo.

A NUCLEAR FAMILY

The closest I ever came was the zoo.
There was the whole mob lying down
at one end of the compound. And one
really big one, the Old Man,
lying on his side, on his elbow
it looked like. With big hind legs
and tail, and funny drooping forepaws
held high in fly-swatting position.
He seemed asleep, but that was only
the look they all have, sleeping or waking,
the eye concealed by the orb
of the big lid curving down . . .
a look of shyness
or some sweet meditation.

But he's not like that, he's a tough one,
Old Man Kangaroo.
I can see him, after the day's work,
standing in the pub with his mates
talking against the Company.
Then, later, reeling home.
As a man walks he creates the road,
the moon gliding above the housetops
and the shadows.

When he comes in, there's his Missus
in the kitchen, lip curled in scorn.
He decides to brazen it out
(a veteran he of many night sorties). . . .
"Let's ha'e a bit o' dinner, then.
I'm about clammed."

She flares up. "Wheer's my money?
Wheer do I come in?
You've had a good jaunt,
tea waiting and washed up,
then you come crawling in.

You suppose, do you, I'm going to keep house for you
while you make a holiday?
You must think something of yourself."

"Don't be gettin thysen in a roar,"
he says, retreating at once, like a veteran.
He pulls a knotted kerchief out of his moleskin
and unties it with miner's fingers,
clumsy from the pick-work.

"Here's thy blessed money,
thy shillings an thy sixpences,"
pouring it on the table.
Then he reaches a hand to her shoulder,
"Now gie us summat, gie us a kiss."

"Behave thysen," she says, pushing him away,
"the child'll see."

"What child?" He looks around. "What?
Is the dear everywhere? I don't see him.
Are his eyes in the wall?"

"Enow o' thy clatter.
I never seen a rip as th'art.
Shall y'ave your dinner warmed?"

"Ay," he says, "an wi' a smite o' cheese."

The members of the family are not speaking "Australian," nor did I mean
them to, a fact that escaped one reviewer in Sydney—he said I had misrep-
resented the language. These kangaroos are speaking English as it used to be
spoken in Nottinghamshire. The author of Kangaroo and the poem about
the mother kangaroo with "her little loose hands, and drooping Victorian
shoulders," is held in high esteem by the race of marsupials.

L.S.

A BUSH BAND

A guitar and drum,
a pole with bottlecaps nailed to it . . .

struck with a piece of wood
it gives off a silvery, joyful sound.

The woman playing the guitar
is sinewy, like the men in the ballad.

Driving their cattle overland
from Broome to Glen Garrick . . .

Cows low, wagon wheels turn,
red dust hangs in the air.

Some give their lives to cattle
and some to the words of a song,

arriving together at Glen Garrick
and at the end of the song.

DEATH OF THUNDERBOLT

Here he came to a place where two creeks meet,
a gouge in the earth, dry rocks ...
yet when it rains it can drown you.

Barren and desolate, unless you're an aborigine
when every rock hides the spirit
of one of your departed relatives.

And for those who know the story
there is the figure of Constable Walker
in the saddle, looking down
at Fred Ward, known as Thunderbolt.

Ward is halfway across the creek
on foot, having released his horse
so as to double back to it later.
An old trick of the bushranger ...
but the constable isn't having any,
he's caught up with Thunderbolt at last.

While parrots flutter in a tree
and a kookaburra laughs like a maniac,
Ward speaks. "Are you a policeman?"
"I am," says Walker. "You surrender."
Then Ward says, "Have you a family?"
to which the constable answers,
"I thought of that before I came here."
And he says again, "You surrender."
"I'll die first," says Ward.

Then the constable, raising his revolver
and shouting "You and I for it!"
struck spur to his horse.

But the beast missed its footing
almost throwing him down.
Ward ran forward and grabbed him by the arm ...
the constable pressed the muzzle of the revolver
against Ward's body, and fired.
Ward attempted to grasp him again ...
the constable struck him over the head
with the butt of the revolver. And Ward fell.

Walker stood, to recover his breath,
then lifted Ward under the arms
and half carried, half dragged him onto the bank.
The bushranger's eyes were closed
and there was a stain on his shirt
where the bullet had gone in.

Scarcely believing what had happened,
it all happened so fast,
his own actions appearing like a dream,
the constable mounted and rode back to Uralla.

Where the Coachwood and Cedar Motor Hotel
now stands, at the head of a street
full of shops and offices where men sit
counting money.

But at dusk when the lights shine on
in the little streets and the surrounding hills,
what would the children do without a story?

Getting to his feet, walking back
to his horse that whinnies in a shadow...
He climbs in the saddle and rides
into the bush where he still lives.

ARMIDALE

The window propped with a nail, gazing across a valley, tawny, with occasional trees, dark green exotics and a crown of gum trees, olive-green and gray against the tawny, lion-skinned earth . . .

The gum trees are "dying back." Some woods appear to have been shelled—there are only white trunks and naked branches. No one seems to know the reason. Some say it's the Christmas beetle—where trees are sparse the beetles concentrate on the trees that are left and consume the foliage. So that more trees die.

The morning air is fresh, the sky light blue without a cloud. We are in the middle of April—Autumn at the antipodes. Where have I felt this quality of the atmosphere, this coolness together with an unclouded sky? In the South of France thirty years ago. The landscape, however, was different, with terraces and rows of vines. The veranda gazed on a sparkling blue sea, the shallows streaked with red. There were flowers, a garden full of flowers. And poppies along the road.

The years between are wiped out by memory. Once again the novelist of the "madeleine" comes to mind: a taste or sensation repeated after an interval of years will return you to the first time you had it, so that the years disappear. Memory walks onto the stage and lifts the hills and carries them away. One is left with the naked stage.

The coast of the South of France brings another in its train. I am in Jamaica, by the pool at Bournemouth, reading Proust for the first time. Wandering in the Guermantes Way I am oblivious to the swaying palms and the waves breaking along the shore. At sixteen I didn't give a damn for the nature that attended me everywhere, Wordsworth's tireless nurse, arching me over with her blue sky in which a mass of white clouds were heaped, fresh from the laundry. I would much rather have had Gloria to look at or Peter to talk to.

I don't know that I've changed: I still want human company. But now I look at nature with a thoughtful eye. The sheer persistence of her behavior strikes me as having some significance behind it. Why do the fields keep returning in their colors, tawny or green? These shining skies . . . it's as though they

156

were saying, Look at us! Consider the light on sea and land. It is what remains.

But people walk around on the surface of the earth, under the sky, without taking notice of it. Not once do they consider the earth and the wonders thereof. They don't give a hoot about nature.

I suppose this is understandable. Nature isn't a kindly nurse. In Australia when you walk into the scene that looked fine at a distance, you are attacked by flies. They get into your ears and eyes. The fields are dry, the foliage monotonous—it takes a practised eye to find variety in gum trees. Yet this is good cattle and sheep grazing country. Think what it is like in the interior! The middle of Australia is a great emptiness.

This may account for the pessimism of the Australian and his tendency to "knock"—the deeper in, the worse it gets. In America from the beginning when people were dissatisfied they were able to move to a better place. But there is no better place in Australia—the first was best, around the edge, where colonies were planted. Outback is desert and rocks. The Australian psyche answers to this geography. People don't want to venture inland—they don't want to explore the Unconscious, they know it will be a desert. They cling to the coastal rim and towns. They stand elbow to elbow in the public bar and stupefy their senses with beer. They are satisfied with betting on horses or watching football on TV.

There once was a race that knew how to live in the interior. The aborigine walked from one watering place to another. He knew a tree that gushed water when you tapped it, and where springs ran underground. He would walk to a place where herbs were coming into harvest, and stay there a while, then walk to another place. He knew how to set fire to the trunks of trees so that plants would grow. This was an exact science: the fire could be set only in the one month out of twelve—at any other time, firing trees would wipe out the crop.

The Outback was not a wilderness to the aborigine—the spirits of his ancestors were there. They had to be propitiated and consulted. From puberty until middle age the male aborigine was engaged in rites of passage: he walked about like a scholar at the University of Gottingen, with extreme caution and a sense of a very thick, multilayered culture. If anything,

157

the lives of these people were too steeped in culture. A mistake could have fatal consequences: the aborigine who, without being licensed to do so, discovered the hiding-places of the tablets of the tribe, and looked upon and handled them, could expect to be put to death.

The white man saw all this walking about as shiftlessness. He fenced the aborigine off from his burying grounds and broke his connection with the spirits. He prevented him from getting at the food he liked, and when the aborigine stole a sheep, the white man branded him a criminal, put him in chains, and shipped him to a prison where he died. He chopped him up and fed his flesh to the dogs. Then the white man was left with a great emptiness to confront, the Australian desert.

But he doesn't confront it. He puts his head down and mends his fences. He argues about the Union—shorter hours and better pay. The rest of his time is given to distractions.

I am not accusing the Australian—he is the white man everywhere, flourishing on the outside and empty within. This continent is like a projection of our inner state. We are all clinging to the edge and asking for distractions. Australia is like a screen on which we see the deserts of the psyche in an age of mass-production.

Far from criticizing the Australian, we may admire those who, in this harsh environment, have had significant lives. Daisy Bates, for example ... in her leg-o'-mutton sleeves and long Victorian skirt and veil of mosquito netting. Daisy lived among the aborigines and was privy to their secrets. She shared her food with them and nursed them when they were sick. Daisy was a secular saint; very few people could live as she did, with no separation between "real life" and the life of the mind.

This is not what the future appears to hold for the rest of us. In his novel *Voss,* Patrick White suggests what may actually happen. The hero and heroine, being far apart from each other, and increasingly removed from pleasure in their own physical existence—he is exploring the wilderness and she is living among middle-class people in Melbourne—construct images of each other in their heads. As their lives become less physical, these images appear more real.

If we cannot live with nature as they used to in Devon, then the answer may be to do without nature and construct im-

158

ages and address ourselves to them. It is the hermetic idea: after all we are what we think we are—our bodies are not very permanent. The answer may be to live in a fantasy.

I am not looking forward to it. I don't want to live "against nature" like a Symbolist or a Surrealist. But as bureaucracy triumphs over every foot of the earth's surface, and men go to their labor like ants, and huddle in multi-level buildings above the ground or in tunnels beneath it, they may have to find their happiness in illusions. There will be generations that have never touched a leaf. Millions of people in the United States are already living this way.

But whereas the Symbolists and Surrealists created their illusions, in the future illusions will be provided. The masses will sit gazing at pictures of green hills and breaking waves, with the appropriate sounds. They won't even have to applaud— they will hear the sound of applause. Access to the real thing will be prohibited to all but a few thousand members of the ruling political party.

The alternative is for our space-explorers to come upon a habitable planet, some place of green earth and clear water, within navigable distance.

VII

RECAPITULATIONS

SUMMER STORM

In that so sudden summer storm they tried
Each bed, couch, closet, carpet, car-seat, table,
Both river banks, five fields, a mountain side,
Covering as much ground as they were able.

A lady, coming on them in the dark
In a white fixture, wrote to the newspapers
Complaining of the statues in the park.
By Cupid, but they cut some pretty capers!

The envious oxen in still rings would stand
Ruminating. Their sweet incessant ploughs
I think had changed the contours of the land
And made two modest conies move their house.

God rest them well, and firmly shut the door.
Now they are married Nature breathes once more.

A WOMAN TOO WELL REMEMBERED

Having put on new fashions, she demands
New friends. She trades her beauty and her humor
In anybody's eyes. If diamonds
Were dark, they'd sparkle so. Her aura is
The glance of scandal and the speed of rumor.

One day, as I recall, when we conversed
In kisses, it amused her to transmit
"What hath God wrought!" — the message that was first
Sent under the Atlantic. Nonsense, yet
It pleases me sometimes to think of it.

Noli me tangere was not her sign.
Her pilgrim trembled with the softest awe.
She was the only daughter of a line
That sleeps in poetry and silences.
She might have sat upon the Sphinx's paw.

Then is she simply false, and falsely fair?
(The promise she would break she never made)
I cannot say, but truly can compare,
For when the stars move like a steady fire
I think of her, and other faces fade.

THE MAN WHO MARRIED MAGDALENE

The man who married Magdalene
Had not forgiven her.
God might pardon every sin ...
Love is no pardoner.

Her hands were hollow, pale and blue,
Her mouth lke watered wine.
He watched to see if she were true
And waited for a sign.

It was old harlotry, he guessed,
That drained her strength away,
So gladly for the dark she dressed,
So sadly for the day.

Their quarrels made her dull and weak
And soon a man might fit
A penny in the hollow cheek
And never notice it.

At last, as they exhausted slept,
Death granted the divorce,
And nakedly the woman leapt
Upon that narrow horse.

But when he woke and woke alone
He wept and would deny
The loose behavior of the bone
And the immodest thigh.

MARIA ROBERTS

In the kingdom of heaven
there is neither past nor future,
but thinking, which is always present.

So it is, at this moment
I am sitting with Maria Roberts
and her young brother, Charles,
in a tram in the South Camp Road.

We are going to the Carib Theater.
But first we shall have to wait
for the tram coming in the other direction.
It seems that we shall spend eternity

staring at the nearest roofs,
trees with the bark shelling off—
eucalyptus—
a hedge that is powdered with dust.

Specks in the sky slowly circling . . .
crows. They seem to hang there.
Like Charley . . . he was shot down
over Germany during the war.

But Maria . . . in the Uffizi
the slender golden Venus,
gray eyes that gaze back at me . . .
must be living still somewhere.

The tram comes around the corner
finally, clanging its gong,
and passes . . . rows of dresses
and trousers and straw hats.

In the last row, the old women
with clay pipes stuck in their teeth
and baskets packed with vegetables
at their feet . . . Going to market.

Then our motorman climbs down
and throws the switch with his pole,
and we're off again, to the theater.
Today they're playing "The Firefly."

In the kingdom of heaven
there is neither past nor future,
but thinking, which is always present:

specks in the sky slowly circling,
a hedge that is covered with dust.

WORKING LATE

A light is on in my father's study.
"Still up?" he says, and we are silent,
looking at the harbor lights,
listening to the surf
and the creak of coconut boughs.

He is working late on cases.
No impassioned speech! He argues from evidence,
actually pacing out and measuring,
while the fans revolving on the ceiling
winnow the true from the false.

Once he passed a brass curtain rod
through a head made out of plaster
and showed the jury the angle of fire—
where the murderer must have stood.
For years, all through my childhood,
if I opened a closet ... bang!
There would be the dead man's head
with a black hole in the forehead.

All the arguing in the world
will not stay the moon.
She has come all the way from Russia
to gaze for a while in a mango tree
and light the wall of a veranda,
before resuming her interrupted journey
beyond the harbor and the lighthouse
at Port Royal, turning away
from land to the open sea.

Yet, nothing in nature changes, from that day to this,
she is still the mother of us all.
I can see the drifting offshore lights,
black posts where the pelicans brood.

And the light that used to shine
at night in my father's study
now shines as late in mine.

PETER

1

At the end of the lane a van moving slowly ...
a single tree like a palm rising above the rest ...
so this is all there is to it,
your long-sought happiness.

2

On winter nights when the moon
hung still behind some scaffolding
you thought, "Like a bird in a cage."
You were always making comparisons ...
"finding similitudes in dissimilars,"
says Aristotle. A form of insanity ...
Nothing is ever what it appears to be,
but always like something else.

3

One has been flung down with its roots in the air.
Another tilts at an angle.
One has lost a limb in the storm
and stands with a white wound.
And one, covered with vines,
every May puts out a mass of flowers.

4

Poetry, says Baudelaire, is melancholy:
the more we desire, the more we shall have to grieve.
Devour a corpse with your eyes; art consists
in the cultivation of pain.
Stupidity reassures you; you do not belong
in a bourgeois establishment, it can never be your home.
Restlessness is a sign of intelligence;
revulsion, the flight of a soul.

ISLAND

Driven by the wind, black billows
surge, and the sand is littered.
Deep, deep in the interior
the temple of the god is hidden.

On slopes overgrown with vines
and thorns, where bees are humming,
with wide, complacent eyes
the wooden face stares calmly.

FROGS

The storm broke, and it rained,
And water rose in the pool,
And frogs hopped into the gutter,

With their skins of yellow and green,
And just their eyes shining above the surface
Of the warm solution of slime.

At night, when fireflies trace
Light-lines between the trees and flowers
Exhaling perfume,

The frogs speak to each other
In rhythm. The sound is monstrous,
But their voices are filled with satisfaction.

In the city I pine for the country;
In the country I long for conversation—
Our happy croaking.

AMERICAN POETRY

Whatever it is, it must have
A stomach that can digest
Rubber, coal, uranium, moons, poems.

Like the shark, it contains a shoe.
It must swim for miles through the desert
Uttering cries that are almost human.

BEFORE THE POETRY READING

*Composition for Voices, Dutch Banjo, Sick
Flute, and a Hair Drum.*

1

This is the poetry reading.
This is the man who is going to give the poetry reading.
He is standing in a street in which the rain is falling
With his suitcase open on the roof of a car for some reason,
And the rain falling into the suitcase,
While the people standing nearby say,
"If you had come on a Monday,
Or a Tuesday, or a Thursday,
If you had come on a Wednesday,
Or on any day but this,
You would have had an audience,
For we here at Quinippiac (Western, or Wretched State U.)
Have wonderful audiences for poetry readings."
By this time he has closed the suitcase
And put it on the back seat, which is empty,
But on the front seat sit Saul Bellow,
James Baldwin, and Uncle Rudy and Fanya.
They are upright, not turning their heads, their fedoras straight on,
For they know where they are going,
And you should know, so they do not deign to answer
When you say, "Where in Hell is this car going?"
Whereupon, with a leap, slamming the door shut,
Taking your suitcase with it, and your Only Available Manuscript,
And leaving you standing there,
The car leaps into the future,
Still raining, in which its taillight disappears.
And a man who is still looking on
With his coat collar turned up, says
"If you had come on a Friday,
A Saturday or a Sunday,
Or if you had come on a Wednesday
Or a Tuesday, there would have been an audience.
For we here at Madagascar
And the University of Lost Causes
Have wonderful audiences for poetry readings."

173

2

This is the man who is going to introduce you.
He says, "Could you tell me the names
Of the books you have written.
And is there anything you would like me to say?"

3

This is the lady who is giving a party for you
After the poetry reading.
She says, "I hope you don't mind, but
I have carefully avoided inviting
Any beautiful, attractive farouche young women;
But the Vicar of Dunstable is coming,
Who is over here this year on an exchange program,
And the Calvinist Spiritual Chorus Society,
And all the members of the Poetry Writing Workshop."

4

This is the man who has an announcement to make.
He says, "I have a few announcements.
First, before the poetry reading starts,
If you leave the building and walk rapidly
Ten miles in the opposite direction,
A concert of music and poetry is being given
By Wolfgang Amadeus Mozart and William Shakespeare.
Also, during the intermission
There is time for you to catch the rising
Of the Latter Day Saints at the Day of Judgement.
Directly after the reading,
If you turn left, past the Community Building,
And walk for seventeen miles,
There is tea and little pieces of eraser
Being served in the Gymnasium.
Last week we had a reading by Dante,
And the week before by Sophocles;
A week from tonight, Saint Francis of Assisi
        will appear in person—
But tonight I am happy to introduce
Mister Willoughby, who will make the introduction
Of our guest, Mr. . . . ."

174

THINGS

A man stood in the laurel tree
Adjusting his hands and feet to the boughs.
He said, "Today I was breaking stones
On a mountain road in Asia,

When suddenly I had a vision
Of mankind, like grass and flowers,
The same over all the earth.
We forgave each other; we gave ourselves
Wholly over to words.
And straightway I was released
And sprang through an open gate."

I said, "Into a meadow?"

He said, "I am impervious to irony.
I thank you for the word. . . .
I am standing in a sunlit meadow.
Know that everything your senses reject
Springs up in the spiritual world."

I said, "Our scientists have another opinion.
They say, you are merely phenomena."

He said, "Over here they will be angels
Singing, Holy holy be His Name!
And also, it works in reverse.
Things which to us in the pure state are mysterious,
Are your simplest articles of household use—
A chair, a dish, and meaner even than these,
The very latest inventions.
Machines are the animals of the Americans—
Tell me about machines."

I said, "I have suspected
The Mixmaster knows more than I do,
The air conditioner is the better poet.
My right front tire is as bald as Odysseus—
How much it must have suffered!

Then, as things have a third substance
Which is obscure to both our senses,
Let there be a perpetual coming and going
Between your house and mine."

ON A DISAPPEARANCE OF THE MOON

And I, who used to lie with the moon,
am here in a peat-bog.

With a criminal, an adulterous girl,
and a witch tied down with branches . . .

the glaucous eyeballs gleaming
under the lids, some hairs still on the chin.

SACRED OBJECTS

1

I am taking part in a great experiment—
whether writers can live peacefully in the suburbs
and not be bored to death.

As Whitman said, an American muse
installed amid the kitchen ware.
And we have wonderful household appliances ...
now tell me about the poets.

Where are your children, Lucina?
Since Eliot died and Pound
has become ... an authority,
chef d'école au lieu d'être tout de go,

I have been listening to the whispers
of U.S. Steel and Anaconda:
"In a little while it will stiffen ...
blown into the road,

drifting with the foam of chemicals."

2

The light that shines through the *Leaves*
is clear: "to form individuals."

A swamp where the seabirds brood.
When the psyche is still and the soul does nothing,
a Sound, with shining tidal pools and channels.

And the kingdom is within you ...
the hills and all the streams
running west to the Mississippi.
There the roads are lined with timothy
and the clouds are tangled with the haystacks.

Your loves are a line of birth trees.
When the wind flattens the grass, it
shines, and a butterfly
writes dark lines on the air.

There are your sacred objects,
the wings and gazing eyes
of the life you really have.

3

Where then shall we meet?

Where you left me.

At the drive-in restaurant ...
the fields on either side covered with stubble,
an odor of gasoline and burning asphalt,
glare on tinted glass, chrome-plated hubcaps and bumpers.

I came out, wiping my hands
on my apron, to take your orders.
Thin hands, streaked with mustard,
give us a hot-dog,
give us a Pepsi-Cola.

Listening to the monotonous grasshoppers
for years I have concentrated on the moment.

And at night when the passing headlights hurl
shadows flitting across the wall,
I sit in a window, combing my hair
day in day out.

THE FLEET FOR TSUSHIMA

Now we're at sea, like the Russians
In the days of the last Tsars.

The houses of stucco gleaming
Adrift in a fog,

The villas of redwood and glass
And the masts of trees and telephone poles

Are like the fleet for Tsushima;
Now they're mournfully leaving

To sail round the world, to explode
And sink in hideous steam.

Darkening the trees and rooftops
The sailors utter terrible cries.

PORT JEFFERSON

My whole life coming to this place,
and understanding it better
maybe for having been born
offshore, and at an early age
left to my own support ...

I have come where sea and wind,
wave and leaf, are one sighing,
where the house strains at an anchor
and the salt-rose clings and clambers
on the humorous grave.

This is the place, Camerado,
that hides the sea-bird's nest.
Listening to the distant voices
in summer, a murmur of the sea,
I seem to remember everything.

THE FOGGY LANE

The houses seem to be floating
in the fog, like lights at sea.

Last summer I came here with a man
who spoke of the ancient Scottish poets—
how they would lie blindfolded,
with a stone placed on the belly,
and so compose their panegyrics . . .
while we, being comfortable, find nothing to praise.

Then I came here with a radical
who said that everything is corrupt;
he wanted to live in a pure world.

And a man from an insurance company
who said that I needed "more protection."

Walking in the foggy lane
I try to keep my attention fixed
on the uneven, muddy surface . . .
the pools made by the rain,
and wheel-ruts, and wet leaves,
and the rustling of small animals.

SEARCHING FOR THE OX

1

I have a friend who works in a mental hospital.
Sometimes he talks of his patients.
There is one, a schizophrenic:
she was born during the Korean War
and raised on an Air Force base.
Then the family moved to La Jolla.
At fourteen she started taking speed
because everyone else was taking it.

Father, I too have my cases:
hands, eyes, voices, ephemera.
They want me to see how they live.
They single me out in a crowd, at a distance,
the one face that will listen
to any incoherent, aimless story.
Then for years they hang around—
"Hey listen!"—tugging at a nerve.
Like the spirits Buddhists call
"hungry ghosts." And when they sense an opening,
rush in. So they are born
and live. So they continue.

There is something in disorder that calls to me.
Out there beyond the harbor
where, every night, the lighthouse
probes the sea with its feathery beam,
something is rising to the surface.
It lies in the darkness breathing,
it floats on the waves regarding
this luminous world,
lights that are shining round the shoreline.
It snorts and splashes,
then rolls its blackness like a tube
back to the bottom.

At dusk when the lamps go on
I have stayed outside and watched

smoke drifts over the rooftops,
and at night the lighted streets go sailing.

At night the gods come down—
the earth then seems so pleasant.
They pass through the murmuring crowd.
They are seen in the cafés and restaurants.
They prefer the voice of a child
or the face of a girl to their fame
in their high, cold palaces on Olympus.

In the evening the wind blows from the sea.
The wind rises and winds like a serpent
filling the diaphanous curtains
where the women sit: Mousmé,
Hélène, and the English girl.
When you pass, their lips make a sound,
twittering, like the swallows
in Cyprus that built their nests
in the temple, above the door.
Each one has a sweetheart far away.
They are making their trousseaux;
they don't make love, they knit.

In the bar down the street
a door keeps opening and closing.
Then a pair of heels go hurrying.
In the streets that lead down to the harbor
all night long there are footsteps
and opening doors. It is Eros
Peridromos, who never sleeps till dawn.

5

Following in the Way
that "regards sensory experience as relatively
    unimportant,"
and that aims to teach the follower
"to renounce what one is attached to" —
in spite of this dubious gift
that would end by negating poetry altogether,
in the practice of meditating

186

on the breath, I find my awareness
of the world—the cry of a bird,
susurrus of tires, the wheezing
of the man in the chair next to me—
has increased. That every sound
falls like a pebble into a well,
sending out ripples that seem to be continuing
through the universe. Sound has a tail
that whips around the corner;
I try not to follow. In any case
I find I am far more aware
of the present, sensory life.

I seem to understand what the artist
was driving at; every leaf stands clear
and separate. The twig seems to quiver
with intellect. Searching for the ox
I come upon a single hoofprint.
I find the ox, and tame it,
and lead it home. In the next scene
the moon has risen, a cool light,
both the ox and herdsman vanished.

There is only earth:
in winter laden with snow,
in summer covered with leaves.

MAGRITTE SHAVING

How calm the torso of a woman,
like a naked statue ...
her right leg painted blue,
her left leg colored saffron.
In an alcove ... The window yields
a view of earth, yellow fields.

*

Objects that you may hold loom large:
a wine-glass, a shaving brush.
The furniture in the room is small:
a bed, a closet with mirrors ...
in the room without walls
in the sky full of clouds.

*

The sphere, colored orange, floating in space
has a face with fixed brown eyes.
Below the sphere, a shirt with a tie
in a dark, formal suit
stands facing you, close to the parapet
on the edge of the canyon.

OUT OF SEASON

Once I stayed at the Grand Hotel
at Beaulieu, on the Mediterranean.
This was in May. A wind blew steadily
from sea to land, banging the shutters.
Now and then a tile would go sailing.

At lunch and dinner we ate fish soup
with big, heavy spoons.
Then there would be fish, then the main course.

At the next table sat an old woman
and her companion, Miss O'Shaughnessy
who was always writing letters
on the desk in the lounge provided for that purpose—
along with copies of *Punch* and *The Tatler*
and an old wind-up Victrola.

There was a businessman from Sweden
and his secretary. She had a stunning figure
on the rocks down by the sea.
She told me, "My name is Helga.
From Vasteras ... " brushing her hair,
leaning to the right, then to the left.

Also, an Englishman who looked ill
and went for walks by himself.

*

I remember a hotel in Kingston
where our mother used to stay
when she came on one of her visits
from America. It was called
the Manor House. There was a long veranda
outside our rooms, and peacocks on the lawn.

We played badminton and golf,
and went swimming at Myrtle Bank.
I did jigsaw puzzles, and water colors,
and read the books she had brought.

In the lounge there were newspapers
from America ... "Gas House Gang Conquer Giants."
What I liked were the cartoons,
"The Katzenjammer Kids" and "Bringing Up Father."

*

Getting back to Beaulieu ...
this could have been one of the places
where the Fitzgeralds used to stay—
the bedroom thirty feet across,
a ceiling twelve feet high.
The bathroom, also, was enormous.

A voice would say ... "Avalon,"
followed by the sound of an orchestra,
and ... shuffling. This would continue
all night, till two or three,
when the last pair of feet went away.

I was preparing to shave
when an arm came out of the wall.
It was holding a tennis racket.
It waved it twice, moved sideways,
flew up, and vanished though the ceiling.

*

Of course not. Yet, it's weird
how I remember the banging shutters
and the walk to the village
past cork trees and slopes lined with vines.

Narrow, cobbled streets going down to the sea ...
There would be boats drawn up, and nets
that a fisherman was always mending.

I sat at a table overlooking the Mediterranean.
At the next table sat the Englishman
who looked unwell. I nodded.

He paid for his drink abruptly
and strode away. Terrified
that I might want his company.

*

At times like this, when I am away from home
or removed in some other way,
it is as though there were another self
that is waiting to find me alone.

Whereupon he steps forward:
"Here we are again, you and me ...
and sounds ... the chirping of birds
and whispering of leaves,
the sound of tires passing on the road."

Yes, and images ... Miss O'Shaughnessy
shouting "Fish soup!" in the old woman's ear.
The businessman from Vasteras
and his girl ... lying on her side,
the curve of her body
from head to slender feet.

The Englishman walking ahead of me ...
He has a stick; as he walks
he slashes with it at the reeds
that are growing beside the road.

These things make an unforgettable impression,
as though there were a reason for being here,
in one place rather than another.

PHYSICAL UNIVERSE

He woke at five and, unable
to go back to sleep,
went downstairs.

A book was lying on the table
where his son had done his homework.
He took it into the kitchen,
made coffee, poured himself a cup,
and settled down to read.

"There was a local eddy in the swirling gas
of the primordial galaxy,
and a cloud was formed, the protosun,
as wide as the present solar system.

This contracted. Some of the gas
formed a diffuse, spherical nebula,
a thin disk, that cooled and flattened.
Pulled one way by its own gravity,
the other way by the sun,
it broke, forming smaller clouds,
the protoplanets. Earth
was 2000 times as wide as it is now."

The earth was without form, and void,
and darkness was upon the face of the deep.

*

"Then the sun began to shine,
dispelling the gases and vapors,
shrinking the planets, melting earth,
separating iron and silicate
to form the core and mantle.
Continents appeared ..."

history, civilisation,
the discovery of America
and the settling of Green Harbor,
bringing us to Tuesday, the seventh of July.

Tuesday, the day they pick up the garbage!
He leaped into action,
took the garbage bag out of its container,
tied it with a twist of wire,
and carried it out to the tool-shed,
taking care not to let the screen-door slam,
and put it in the large garbage-can
that was three-quarters full.
He kept it in the tool-shed so the raccoons
couldn't get at it.

He carried the can out to the road,
then went back into the house
and walked around, picking up newspapers
and fliers for: "Thompson Seedless Grapes,
California's finest sweet eating";

"Scott Bathroom Tissue";

"Legislative report from Senator Ken LaValle."

He put all this paper in a box,
and emptied the waste baskets in the two
downstairs bathrooms,
and the basket in the study.

He carried the box out to the road,
taking care not to let the screen-door slam,
and placed the box next to the garbage.

Now let the garbage men come!

   *

He went back upstairs.
Susan said, "Did you put out the garbage?"
But her eyes were closed.
She was sleeping, yet could speak in her sleep,
ask a question, even answer one.

"Yes," he said, and climbed into bed.
She turned around to face him,
with her eyes still closed.

He thought, perhaps she's an oracle,
speaking from the Collective Unconscious.
He said to her, "Do you agree with Darwin
that people and monkeys have a common ancestor?
Or should we stick to the Bible?"

She said, "Did you take out the garbage?"

"Yes," he said, for the second time.
Then thought about it. Her answer
had something in it of the sublime.
Like a *koan* ... the kind of irrelevance
a Zen-master says to the disciple
who is asking riddles of the universe.

He put his arm around her,
and she continued to breathe evenly
from the depths of sleep.

THE SOUND OF WORDS FOR THEIR OWN SAKE—

AN AFTERWORD

"Come back to the ways things used to be," says the TV commercial. "Make it Jamaica. Again!" I have mixed feelings about this. I am the other Jamaican, a child of the middle class, some of us white, some "colored," but all of us borrowing our manners and prejudices from the English. We had servants, and tea was served every afternoon on the veranda at four o'clock. After the Second World War, Jamaica was made independent of Britain. I am sure Jamaicans don't want things to be the way they used to be.

My father, Aston, was a native. His family went back to Scotland, and there was a Frenchman mixed up in it somewhere. Aston was a lawyer, and he had an older brother, also a lawyer, who had been mayor of Kingston. During the earthquake of 1907 Uncle Bertie lost a leg and was known thereafter as Corkfoot. At election time the calypso singers had a song about him:

> Corkfoot Simpson yuh vagabon'
> an if ah ketch yuh ah chop off de odder one.

My mother was born in Russia. She came to New York with her family when she was a young girl and went to work in the garment district. Then she became an actress, in silent movies. There was an opening for a young woman in Annette Kellerman's company of bathing beauties. My mother tried out for the part. The test was to jump into a tank full of water and act as though she were drowning. She jumped and gave a convincing performance, for she couldn't swim a stroke, and when they pulled her out she was hired.

The bathing beauties came to Jamaica to make a movie called *Neptune's Daughter* and stayed at the Myrtle Bank Hotel in Kingston. My father and some other unmarried men went to have a look at them. Then my mother fell out with the director. He wanted his beauties to pose in the nude. My mother and another young woman refused, and they were given their tickets back to New Yok. My father went there to court her, and they were married. He brought her back to Jamaica, and they set up housekeeping near Cross Roads in the middle-class style. My mother handed the tea cups around and joined the Liguanea Club, but she did not fit in. She was far too emotional.

197

I trace my beginnings as a writer to the stories my mother read to me—Oscar Wilde's "The Happy Prince" was one of her favorites—and the stories she told about her childhood in Russia. She spoke of Cossacks and wolves, of freezing in winter, and rats. In Volhynia rats carried the typhus bacilli that had killed her sister Lisa and almost killed her.

My love of stories became a family joke. When one of my mother's sisters came from New York to stay with us for a while, the first thing I would say was "Tell me a story." And when she had finished, "Tell me another."

I also went to the garden boy for anything I could get out of him. The garden boy clipped the hedges and watered the flowers. He rolled the tennis court, and when there were lawn-tennis parties he ran about and returned the balls. When my father went bird shooting, the garden boy went along to retrieve the birds. When my father obtained a motor launch and took us out in the harbor on Sundays, the garden boy served as an able seaman.

I speak of a garden boy, but there were several. They came and went, dismissed for some infraction of the rules. I tested them all to find if they had any stories. It was Nancy stories I was after, tales of Bro'er Nancy—the Daddy Long Legs spider—Bro'er Alligator, Bro'er Tiger, Bro'er Donkey and Bro'er Crow. Some of the stories were frightening. There was one in which Bro'er Alligator's house had a roof made of bones. But Wordsworth tells us that imagination is fostered by fear as well as beauty.

Beautiful the island surely was—the most beautiful island in the world, said H.M. Tomlinson. I remember sunsets viewed from the mountain where I went to school. There was a plain stretching below, and beyond it an empty sea. The plain was arid and as empty as the sea. Over to the west, as night fell, lights began to shine from the settlement at the mouth of Black River.

We were taught by Englishmen. In all our subjects except science and mathematics we were required to write essays. There was English composition, of course, but we also wrote essays on history, geography and Scripture. We translated Latin and French into English sentences. I entered Munro College when I was nine, and eight years later, when I left, I could write on any subject with facility. On one of my report cards, however, the headmaster remarked that I was in danger of becoming too facile—the results were better when I took the time to think. I have heeded the warning: I write sentences over and over, and a poem may go through fifty drafts.

Outside the classroom I read historical novels by G.A. Henty and Erckmann-Chatrian, farcical novels by W.W. Jacobs and P.G. Wodehouse, and novels of romance and adventure. Every Christmas my father gave me the big red *Chums* annual, which was full of stories for boys. There would be a serial about English schoolboys, the kind we were supposed to be. The hero and his friends were manly and straightforward and not too clever, the sort England could depend on. There was a fat boy who was always eating pies and jam and being caned, whereupon he would howl with pain. Great fun! There was an aristrocratic boy with a monocle who said, "Bai Jove!", a dusky boy from India who spoke babu English but was good at cricket, and a bully and his cronies who smoked cigarettes and, you could surmise, had other bad habits.

When I was fourteen I wrote an essay on the coronation of George VI for a competition being held by the *Daily Gleaner*. Having read an article in the same newspaper that described the procession to Westminster Abbey, I let my imagination have free rein and painted a picture of gaily caparisoned horses, gilded coaches, and lords and ladies graciously bowing to an adoring populace. For an original touch I found fault with Shakespeare for some lines he had written saying that a king's life was not all it was cracked up to be. My essay won the first prize and was published in the *Gleaner*. With the five pounds of my prize money, a lot in those days—my weekly allowance was two shillings and sixpence, about fifty cents—I bought a bicycle and went riding all over Kingston, avoiding the tram lines, in lanes shadowed by bamboo and eucalyptus, by hedges powdered with dust. Sometimes I rode by the house where Maria Roberts lived, hoping that she would appear and admit that she was just as much in love with me as I was with her, but this never came to pass.

The next year, I won the second prize in a short-story competition, and this too was published in the *Gleaner*. I wrote about a young man who came from the country to Kingston to find work—as our garden boys did. My protagonist arrived in Kingston just in time for an earthquake. I based my description of the earthquake on the movie *San Francisco,* which had recently been playing at the Carib Theater. I had him save the life of a stranger, who thereupon rewarded him by handing over his wallet. I had not read the Horatio Alger stories but discovered the formula for a hero on my own: a willing disposition and good luck.

My hero returned to his hut in the mountains to find his mother dying. (My mother had divorced my father and gone back to the States—she came back to Jamaica from time to time to see my brother and me.) The story ended with the words, "Too late, too late!"

I had been reading Thomas Hardy. I was also reading novels by Thackeray, Dickens, Austen and Conrad. My cousin Sybil, who worked in the public library in Kingston, tried to dissuade me from taking out a novel by Zola, but she could not actually prevent it. I read modern novels such as *Point Counterpoint* that were said to be risqué. I read D.H. Lawrence and was eyeing the copy of *Ulysses* my brother had got from England by mail order.

I was also reading poetry and trying to write it. In school we were taught Shakespeare, Shelley and Keats, and the "Georgian poets" whom our English masters were fond of because they described English meadows and English birds and beasts. We were required to memorize poems by W.H. Davies, John Masefield and Walter de la Mare.

I discovered A.E. Housman for myself, and for a year or two read his lyrics with the kind of sympathy that a young American now feels for rock. I lay beneath the willows that lined the driveway to the school, reading Housman's ballads about "lads" who were betrayed by "lasses" and killed a rival and were going to swing for it. Or they enlisted in the Lancers and traveled to a foreign land and found a soldier's grave.

Then I discovered the poems of T.S. Eliot. I was becoming sophisticated.

*

My father and Norman Manley would sometimes work together on a case. Manley had studied for the bar in England and married an English woman. In later years he would be the first Prime Minister of Jamaica, and his son Michael would be

Prime Minister in his turn.

Mrs. Manley was one of the extraordinary individuals England produced—along with the stuffed shirts—gifted people who broke through the barriers of their class and education. With her encouragement, a number of young people came together to discuss politics, literature and art. We spoke of the changes that were taking place and looked forward to the day when Jamaica would be independent. As long as we were colonials we would feel, and be, inferior.

I knew very little about politics, but from my reading of the "Oxford poets," W.H. Auden, Louis MacNeice and others, I had imbibed leftist ideas. Moreover, the successes of Hitler and Mussolini drove one to the left. But my writing remained apolitical: poems about trees, and the sea, and a poem about passengers riding in a bus. I published a short story called "In Love and Puberty" that offended my Aunt May—as I recall, she sniffed. These writings came out in a periodical called *Public Opinion*. I was becoming a name, a "writer."

My father had expected me to be a lawyer, but he had died, and it was up to me to decide. There was no question at all in my mind. I wanted to write, and I wanted to get out of Jamaica.

Why? Because I was young and wanted to see the world. It was as simple as that. There was talk of my going to Oxford, but I could only do so if I won a scholarship, and that was most uncertain. Then my mother wrote and asked if I would like to come to New York for a visit. I came and did not go back.

I entered Columbia College, and for some time continued to think of myself as a revolutionary, looking back to my connection with *Public Opinion*. I went to see *Ten Days That Shook the World* at the Stanley Theater and movies in which Joe Stalin puffed benignly on his pipe and patted little children on the head. Over in Germany, Adolf Hitler was also patting little children on the head; but that was Nazism, quite a different thing.

Then I went off to the war, three years of it. I began with the tanks and finished with the 101st Airborne Division. We fought in Normandy, Holland, Belgium and Germany. I came back from the war much changed. To this day when I see an open field I think, How are we going to get across that?

After the war I went back to Columbia and wrote furiously. I wrote short stories, one of which was published by *Esquire*,

201

and a novel without characters or a plot. Then I had what used to be called a "nervous breakdown"—under repeated bombardment my brains had become unhinged. All this writing prose made something snap—they were banging like a loose shutter in the wind.

After some months I came out of it. Columbia College wouldn't have me back, but the School of General Studies would. I took courses there in the evenings. I did the nightshift on the *New York Herald Tribune*. But I had no interest in reporting. I got a job in an import-export firm, packing ballpoint pens and damaged stockings for export to Europe. And I wrote poems.

To write prose you have to be stable, day in day out, and I wasn't stable yet. Besides, my ambition to be a famous writer had been dampened by my breakdown. I no longer had the confidence you need to pour out words, page after page, to create characters, to believe in your own fantasies. It appeared that I would not be a novelist.

But with poetry I could express an idea or tell a story in a brief space, and it would hang together. Besides, I loved the rhythm and the sound of words for their own sake. So I wrote poems about the war and other matters, and when I was twenty-six published my first book, at my own expense. I was living in Paris that year, and I went to a printer and paid him $500 to make 500 copies of my poems. *The Arrivistes* was priced at $2. I sent some copies out for review and gave some away, and the rest were stolen. They still turn up on the market from time to time, looking brand-new, selling for $300.

So I was going to write poems. I hadn't intended this—it was the way I could go. A matter of temperament, and the way the land lay, what I was able to do and what I could not.

From time to time I have asked myself what I hope to accomplish by writing poems. Poetry is of no importance in the United States. The people in the town where I live, who talk to me about the movies or television shows they have seen, do not read my poems. It would not occur to them to buy one of my books. Then who do I write for?

I don't write for myself—what would be the point of that? Writing is hard work—as I've said, it is mostly rewriting. On the other hand, I don't write for the "public." There are writers of verse who manage to reach a fairly wide audience, but I am not gifted that way. In order to have a public I would have to give up writing the kind of poem I like to write. There would be no pleasure in it, any more than there would be in writing for myself.

I write poems in order to express feelings I have had since I was a child. As Wordsworth says, the feelings may not be as spontaneous as they used to be, but years bring a "philosophic mind," and you can express your feelings as you could not when you were a child.

I have always felt that there is a power and intelligence in things. I felt it as a boy when I watched the sun setting from the top of a mountain and rode a bicycle in the lanes of Kingston and walked along the shore, listening to the sea. I felt that power when I first saw Manhattan rise out of the Atlantic, the towers a poet describes as "moody water-loving giants." During the war I felt there was an intelligence watching and listening. Others had expressed their sense of it. When I came upon an old trench of the First World War I remembered the lines by Wilfred Owen:

> *Our brains ache, in the merciless iced east winds that*
> *knive us ...*
> *Wearied we keep awake because the night is silent ...*

Weeks later, in the snow around Bastogne, I could apply these words to myself and my companions. I write poems, as did men and women who lived before me, to express the drama, the terror and beauty of life.

CHRONOLOGY OF THE POEMS

Most of the poems in this book were selected from my previously published books. The following is a detailed chronology of the publication of those poems and books. (L.S.)

The Arrivistes: Poems 1940-1949.
New York. The Fine Editions Press, 1949.

Carentan O Carentan
Rough Winds Do Shake
Summer Storm

Good News of Death and Other Poems. In *Poets of Today II.*
New York. Charles Scribner's Sons, 1955.

As Birds Are Fitted to the Boughs
A Woman Too Well Remembered
Early in the Morning
Memories of a Lost War
The Ash and the Oak
The Battle
The Heroes
The Man Who Married Magdalene
West

A Dream of Governors.
Middletown, Connecticut. Wesleyan University Press, 1959.

A Dream of Governors
Hot Night on Water Street
I Dreamed that in a City Dark as Paris
Old Soldier
The Bird
The Boarder
The Custom of the World
The Goodnight
The Silent Generation
To the Western World

At the End of the Open Road.
Middletown, Connecticut. Wesleyan University Press, 1963.

American Poetry
A Story about Chicken Soup
Birch
Frogs
In California
In the Suburbs
Lines Written near San Francisco
Love, My Machine
My Father in the Night Commanding No
On the Lawn at the Villa
Summer Morning
The Cradle Trap
The Inner Part
The Morning Light
The Redwoods
There Is
The Riders Held Back
The Troika
Walt Whitman at Bear Mountain

Selected Poems.
New York. Harcourt, Brace and World, 1965.

After Midnight
Luminous Night
Outward
Things

Adventures of the Letter I.
New York. Harper & Row, Publishers, 1971.

Adam Yankev
A Friend of the Family
American Dreams
A Night in Odessa
A Son of the Romanovs
Dvonya
Indian Country

Isidor
Island
On a Disappearance of the Moon
On the Eve
Port Jefferson
Sacred Objects
Simplicity
The Climate of Paradise
The Country House
The Foggy Lane
The Peat-Bog Man
The Pihis
The Silent Piano
Trasimeno
Vandergast and the Girl

Searching for the Ox.
New York. William Morrow and Company, Inc., 1976.

Baruch
Before the Poetry Reading
Newspaper Nights
Searching for the Ox
The Hour of Feeling
The Middleaged Man
The Stevenson Poster
The Street

Armidale.
Brockport, New York. BOA Editions, Ltd., 1979.

A Bush Band
A Nuclear Family
Armidale
As a Man Walks
Death of Thunderbolt

Caviare at the Funeral.
New York. Franklin Watts, 1980.

A Bower of Roses
A Bush Band
American Classic
A Nuclear Family
As a Man Walks
A River Running By
Armidale
Back in the States
Caviare at the Funeral
Chocolates
Death of Thunderbolt
Little Colored Flags
Magritte Shaving
Maria Roberts
On the Ledge
Out of Season
Peter
Sway
The Art of Storytelling
The Beaded Pear
The Man She Loved
The Mexican Woman
The Pawnshop
Typhus
Unfinished Life
Why Do You Write about Russia?
Working Late

*

The following poems are previously uncollected:

Physical Universe
Quiet Desperation
The Fleet for Tsushima

INDEX OF TITLES

INDEX OF FIRST LINES

In my grandmother's house there was always chicken soup
In that so sudden summer storm they tried
In the dusk
In the kingdom of heaven
In the morning light a line
In the town of Odessa
Isidor was always plotting
It's a classic American scene—
It's a strange country—
It was cold, and all they gave him to wear
I wake and feel the city trembling.
Lines of little colored flags
Look! From my window there's a view
Love, my machine
Memory rising in the steppes
Mountains are moving, rivers
My father in the night commanding No
My whole life coming to this place,
Neither on horseback nor seated,
Now we're at sea, like the Russians
One morning, as we traveled in the fields
Once I stayed at the Grand Hotel
Once some people were visiting Chekhov.
Once upon a time in California
Once upon a time there was a *shocket*,
On the lawn at the villa—
On the way back from the cemetery
On US 101
O, we loved long and happily, God knows!
Rough winds do shake
Since first I read in *Zone*
Talking to someone your own age
The air was aglimmer, thousands of snowflakes
The closest I ever came was the zoo.
The dark streets were deserted,
The first time I saw a pawnshop
The guns know what is what, but underneath
The houses seem to floating
The Knight from the world's end
The man who married Magdalene

The mixture of smells
There are whole blocks in New York
There is a middleaged man, Tim Flanagan,
There is an old folk saying:
There is something sad about property
There's no way out
The staff slips from the hand
The storm broke, and it rained,
The time is after dinner. Cigarettes
The "villages" begin further out ...
"The whole earth was covered with snow,
The window propped with a nail,
This is Avram the cello-mender
This is the poetry reading
Trees in the old days used to stand
Troike, troika! The snow moon
This prairie light ... I see
Vandergast to his neighbors—
We have lived like civilized people.
Whatever it is, it must have
When Hannibal defeated the Roman army
When Hitler was the Devil
When I was a child
When men discovered freedom first
When they had won the war
You always know what to expect

LOUIS SIMPSON

Louis Simpson is the author of nine books of poetry, including *At the End of the Open Road,* which was awarded the Pulitzer Prize, *Adventures of the Letter I,* and *Caviare at the Funeral.* His poetry has been acclaimed for its superb lyrical and narrative qualities, and for its openness to experience. "Mr. Simpson's poems," said a critic writing in the *Times Literary Supplement,* "make a stand with persistence of life, regaining of vision, against barbarian violence."

Born in the West Indies, the son of a lawyer of Scottish descent and a Russian mother, Louis Simpson emigrated to the United States at the age of seventeen. He studied at Columbia University, then served with the U.S. Army overseas, on active duty in France, Holland, Belgium and Germany. After the war he continued his studies at Columbia and at the University of Paris. While living in France he published his first book of poems, *The Arrivistes.*

He worked as an editor in a publishing house in New York, then obtained the Ph.D. at Columbia and went into teaching. He has taught at Columbia, at the University of California in Berkeley, and since 1967 at the State University of New York at Stony Brook. In 1975 the publication of *Three on the Tower,* a study of Ezra Pound, T.S. Eliot and William Carlos Williams, brought Mr. Simpson wide acclaim as a literary critic. Other works of literary criticism followed: *A Revolution in Taste* and *A Company of Poets.*

Louis Simpson's honors and awards, in addition to the Pulitzer Prize, include the Prix de Rome, Guggenheim Foundation fellowships, and the Medal for Excellence given by Columbia University.

People Live Here: Selected Poems 1949-1983 has been issued in a first edition of three thousand copies, of which one thousand nine hundred and sixty are in paper and one thousand are in cloth. An additional forty copies have been specially bound by Gene Eckert in quarter-cloth and French papers over boards: twenty-five copies, numbered I-XXV and signed, also include a poem in holograph by Louis Simpson; fifteen copies, numbered i-xv and signed by Louis Simpson, have been retained by the publisher for presentation purposes.